The
Big
Book
of Healthy
Cooking Oils

The Big Book

of Healthy

Cooking Oils

Recipes Using Coconut Oil and
Other Unprocessed and Unrefined Oils

Lisa Howard

cooking instructor and culinary speaker

PAGE STREET
PUBLISHING CO.

PAGE STREET
PUBLISHING CO.

Copyright © 2015 Lisa Howard
First published in 2015 by
Page Street Publishing Co.
27 Congress Street, Suite 103
Salem, MA 01970
www.pagestreetpublishing.com

Distributed by Macmillan, sales in Canada by The Canadian Manda Group.

18 17 16 15   1 2 3 4 5

ISBN-13: 9781624141485
ISBN-10: 162414148X

Library of Congress Control Number: 2015934101

Cover and book design by Page Street Publishing Co.
Photography by Jenny Castaneda

Printed and bound in China

Page Street is proud to be a member of 1% for the Planet. Members donate one percent of their sales to one or more of the over 1,500 environmental and sustainability charities across the globe who participate in this program.

To Michael and André, who have been
The Men In My Life for more than a decade.

Thank you for always being there.

Contents

What You'll Find in This Book

Welcome to the world of oils! Unrefined oils, that is: Oils that are aromatic, flavorful and fresh. I'm talking about the kind of oil that offers many health benefits, ranging from anti-inflammatory omega-3 fats in flaxseed and walnut oils to antibacterial and antiviral lauric acid, which is one of the main components of coconut oil. But the best thing about unrefined oils is that each one has a signature flavor. A dollop of ghee tastes so rich and buttery that it can create an instant sauce, while nut oils such as pistachio and almond add delightful accents to everything from salads to stir-frys.

Along with having a unique flavor, each oil also has its own unique use in the kitchen: Some handle heat well and are ideal for speedy high-heat cooking, but then again, others shouldn't be heated at all and are best used in dressings, dips and drizzles. Most oils fall in between, and they are just as happy in medium-heat settings, such as baking and sautéing, as they are in no-heat dishes.

Understanding the basic aspects of oils means you'll be able to fully appreciate all of the unique flavors and abilities of unrefined oils, plus you'll know how to select and store your oils to make sure that you choose the best oils and keep them fresh. It's always a good idea to protect your investments.

In addition to information about unrefined oils and fats, this book also features recipes that are 100 percent gluten-free and made without any refined grains or sweeteners. The recipes are also Paleo-friendly, with substitutions suggested whenever dairy, grain or legume ingredients are included. And if you're diabetic or looking to lose weight, these recipes are perfect for you, too. Emphasizing fresh, unprocessed ingredients with low glycemic impact is a great way to improve your day-to-day health.

Now it's time to explore!

A Note About Animal Products

As part of this cookbook's emphasis on unrefined oils and fats, the recipes also focus on grass-fed animal products. Such products also fall into the category of "unrefined." From a flavor and nutritional standpoint, hamburger meat from a concentrated animal feeding operation (CAFO) steer is not the same as hamburger meat from a grass-fed steer that has been grazing freely and living in open outdoor spaces. Cheese made with milk from grass-fed cows is not the same as processed cheese made with conventional milk. We'll talk more about the anti-inflammatory aspects of grass-fed animal products in the section concerning omega-3 fats. (See page 20.)

Products from animals raised conventionally come from animals that have been given foods they wouldn't normally eat and are living in conditions they wouldn't normally live in. (These animals are often routinely fed antibiotics, growth hormones and genetically modified foods, and they live in extremely crowded conditions that contribute to disease.) It's a far cry indeed from the life of grass-fed cows, free-range chickens and pastured hogs! How animals are raised leads to differences in flavor, optimal cooking techniques and nutritional content, whether we're talking about meat, eggs or dairy products.

When you're shopping for grass-fed animal products, you'll find a cornucopia of terms that may or may not apply to what you're getting. While the standards for organic produce and animal products are firmly established, there isn't yet a legal set of requirements for grass-fed/pastured/free-range/sustainable/wild products. It is worth pointing out, though, that small, independent grocery stores focused on local foods and fresh produce are more likely to stock grass-fed animal products, as are farmers' markets. Other options include purchasing farm shares or cow shares. In those scenarios, you'll be purchasing directly from the farmer.

Note that "organic" in terms of animal products does not mean "grass-fed." The certification organic simply means that the animal is not fed genetically modified foods, growth hormones, or sub-therapeutic antibiotics. That's it. Some farmers who raise grass-fed animals do go to the trouble of also being certified organic; others don't. Your best bet to verify authenticity is to visit the farm, talk to farmers at a nearby farmers' market and/or network with like-minded folks who may already be buying products that are truly farm-fresh and who can recommend farmers to you.

And a final note on the culinary differences between grass-fed and conventional meats: Grass-fed meats are much leaner and therefore cook more quickly than conventional meats do. A good general rule is "half the time, half the heat." If you're used to searing a steak on high for ten minutes, when you upgrade to grass-fed steaks, cook them on medium for five minutes. You can always keep cooking them or turn up the heat, but you can't un-cook an overcooked steak. It's better to be safe than sorry! Free-range eggs, too, cook more quickly than conventional eggs. Because the recipes in this book have been developed with grass-fed meats, you may have to cook your meats longer than specified if you're using conventional meats.

When it comes to dairy products, the biggest difference you'll notice is that whole-milk dairy products are much creamier tasting than conventional products are. Grass-fed cream that hasn't been subjected to ultra-high temperature (UHT) pasteurization whips much faster and higher than conventional cream does. Whole milk frothed for lattes makes more foam. Egg whites whip better and can hold their shape better when they're from free-range hens.

But of course, the biggest difference you'll notice when you start enjoying products from grass-fed animals is the taste. The flavors are so much richer and more satisfying! Don't believe me? Try a strip of pastured bacon.

Oils and Your Health

For decades, fat has gotten a big thumbs-down, while proteins and carbohydrates have been put on culinary pedestals. Lately, though, carbs have taken on a less-than-angelic reputation. Some of them are thought of as being "good" carbs (whole-grain, whole-food products), while others have acquired a reputation for being "bad" carbs (processed, refined products). Protein, too, has come under greater scrutiny because shoppers have come to realize that many products boasting added protein are in fact highly processed foods. The extra protein often consists of soy, dairy and/or wheat ingredients, all of which are common allergens that many people must avoid. Our once black-and-white view of nutrition is becoming complex shades of gray.

So, what *are* these macronutrients, really? And how do they impact our health? Although this book is primarily about fats, let's sketch out the bigger picture so that you can better understand where and how fats fit in. We'll start with protein. It's more clear-cut than carbs and fats.

Proteins

You've probably heard the phrase "complete protein" and wondered what that meant. To back up a step, proteins are made of multiple amino acid chains that our bodies break down to digest. There are roughly twenty amino acids that our bodies use to build cells and muscles and facilitate immune responses. Others act as enzymes that trigger metabolic processes. In a nutshell, protein is essential to the health of every animal on the planet. Fortunately, our bodies can synthesize most of those amino acids. Nine of them, however, can't be synthesized. We have to eat them. We call a food a "complete protein" when it contains all nine of those amino acids.

The vast majority of complete proteins come from animal and seafood/fish sources because they've already had to synthesize those proteins for themselves. Plant foods are rarely complete proteins. (Quinoa, amaranth and soy are notable exceptions.) But the good news is that by strategically overlapping plant foods, we can obtain complete proteins from them. In other words, if you eat a wide variety of plants—and make a special effort to combine certain groups such as legumes and grains—your protein needs will be mostly satisfied. Or you may choose to eat eggs and dairy but not outright meat. Or perhaps you enjoy fish and seafood, or you just garnish your meals with meat occasionally rather than featuring it as the main dish. Eating less meat but focusing on good-quality meat (and fish/seafood) provides us with more accessible protein sources compared with only eating plants, yet fits better with sustainable foodstyles that emphasize treating animals humanely.

Many Americans insist they're not getting enough protein (not often the case), and they fall prey to marketing campaigns that tout products with added protein from processed, potentially allergenic sources, such as soy, dairy or wheat. Downing a milkshake replete with powdered soy and whey (and probably lots of added sugars and artificial flavorings) is not an example of eating high-quality protein. Enjoying a plate of fruit, olives and grass-fed cheeses is. Spinach salad topped with strips of sautéed grass-fed steak is another great example of a complete protein-rich meal. So is wild Alaskan salmon, or a free-range poached egg served *huevos rancheros*–style with fresh salsa. If you stick with protein from natural sources as opposed to industrially added, heavily processed protein powders, you'll have plenty of good-quality protein on your plate.

Carbohydrates

Next up: carbs. Whereas nearly all sources of complete proteins stem from animal and seafood/fish sources, carbs are more readily found in plant foods. When pondering the different types of carbs, it's worth taking note of the macrobiotic principle of upward- and downward-growing plants. Anything that's underneath the soil is usually the storage-storing part of the plant, which means it's the starchy part. Take beets, for example. The bulb is the root, which you can simmer and mash the way you would a potato. The leaves are hearty and green, reminiscent of chard or collards—not starchy at all. Ditto for turnip bulbs and turnip greens. Anything that falls into the downward-growing category of plants is going to be more starchy and break down more quickly into sugar in your bloodstream than most upward-growing plants do.

The giant exceptions to this downward/upward split are grains (which tend to be starchy) and tropical fruits (which have high amounts of natural sugar). But no matter which direction plants grow, they are all whole and unprocessed foods—although some have to be cooked, pounded or otherwise processed before they're edible. These foods are "good" carbs. They're full of fiber, they contain a mélange of vitamins and minerals, and they offer a dizzying array of flavors. These foods are good for you, and they are fun to play with! (Note that you want to focus on upward-growing, non-grain and non-tropical plants if you want to lose weight or are pre-diabetic/diabetic.)

But in the majority of aisles in any grocery store, you'll find "bad" carbs, which is to say processed, refined carbs, most of which are empty sugars in the sense that we expend virtually no energy in breaking them down. They are, in effect, predigested. Think of baby food: It's cooked, mashed and pureed, all in an effort to break the food down as much as possible so that babies can easily access the nutrients in the food. This is great for underdeveloped digestive systems in babies, but it's not a good idea for adults whose digestive systems are meant to have to break down what we eat.

If you eat an apple, for example, you're getting the full nutritional benefits of the apple. But once you've cooked and mashed it into applesauce, you have baby food. Once you've pressed the apple into juice, you have sheer sugar, without any fiber at all and with only a faint suggestion of its former vitamins. You'll also lose the pleasurable satiety of the entire apple. Odds are, you'd just eat one apple (and therefore the natural sugar from just that one apple) and be satisfied, but did you know that *one eight-ounce glass of apple juice contains three to four apples?* Our natural one-apple stopping point is lost in the rush of amped-up sugar from the instantly digested juice.

These processed carbs are the carbs that spike our blood sugar levels, cause obesity, lead to diabetes and inflammation and, in general, cause our health to suffer. Fortunately, in both this book and my *Healthier Gluten-Free* cookbook, all of the recipes contain 100 percent whole-grain, whole-food carbs. Plus the recipes containing sweeteners use natural, less-processed sweeteners that don't break down as quickly as processed sugars do.

Something critical to note about carbs and how they fit into the big health picture is that processed, "bad" carb consumption inevitably increases when people go on low-fat diets. That's because when fat is artificially taken out of a product, the full flavor and luxurious mouthfeel of fat is re-created with sugars, gums and thickeners. Also, because fat and protein are often found together—remember, complete proteins mostly come from animal and seafood/fish sources, which are low in carbs and high in fats compared with plant foods—often good-quality protein disappears as the sugar content goes up. Let's quickly compare whole-milk plain yogurt to nonfat plain yogurt. When the fat is removed, the protein drops in half, and the sugar goes up 50 percent. This is an excellent example of the wise adage "Leave well enough alone!"

Comparing Yogurts

	Fage Total Classic Yogurt (whole-milk): 7 ounces (200 g)	Dannon All-Natural Plain Nonfat Yogurt: 6 ounces (170 g)
Protein	18 g	9 g
Fat	10 g	0 g
Sugar	8 g	12 g

Fats

We've saved the best for last! Now let's talk fats, or at least how they fit into the trio of macronutrients known as fats, proteins and carbs. We'll talk more about how exactly oils and fats are refined in "How Oils Go Bad" (page 19) and what the health effects of the refining process are. We'll also talk more about the specific health attributes of saturated fats as well as polyunsaturated fats in later chapters. For now, let's just cover the basic facts about fats.

Fats are derived from animal as well as plant sources. When they're animal-sourced, fat is packaged with protein. When fats are found in plant foods, they tend to come along with a generous portion of fat-rich, fiber-rich, nutritious carbs. (Think of avocadoes and whole grains.) Some plants are pressed to extract their juices, which we refer to as oil. Olives yield olive oil, peanuts yield peanut oil, flaxseeds yield flax oil, etc.

Fats have always been an integral ingredient on our menu, but they fell out of favor in the United States during the latter half of the twentieth century due to a perfect storm of corporate marketing interests and botched research. The sugar industry in particular stood to benefit from pushing the idea that fat was bad, a notion stemming from the not-necessarily-relevant finding that fats contain nearly twice as many calories as proteins and carbs do. Based on this purely numerical approach, ads ran in popular women's magazines promoting the idea that a tablespoon of refined white sugar was one of the healthiest things you could eat, far healthier than the equivalent portion of extra-virgin olive oil or an apple. After all, the apple has more calories! Never mind the fiber, vitamins, minerals, antioxidants and the other micronutrients an apple offers. The numbers had sugar as the winner.

You'd be hard-pressed to find anyone today who would agree with this idea. The ignore-the-details formula of "calories in, calories out" is starting to be viewed as a concept that applies more to mechanical engineering principles than to the complex, ever-changing fluctuations of human biology.

Happily, more attention is being given to the idea that the quality of the food is just as important—if not more so—than the quantity consumed. Researchers are continually touting the benefits of extra-virgin olive oil, not pomace oil. (The former is unrefined; the latter is the most-processed form of olive oil on the market.) People are being told to drizzle cold-pressed flaxseed oil into their smoothies and onto their salads. Unrefined virgin coconut oil has made it into mainstream grocery stores. But tragically, despite the recent push for better-quality oils, most oils are still sold in their refined, rancid forms rather than as whole, minimally processed oils that retain their beneficial nutrients and delicious flavors.

Before we get into the nitty-gritty of how fats are built and what their individual attributes and benefits are, it's worth shedding light on another misconception: the idea that any given food is a saturated, monounsaturated or polyunsaturated fat. We're in the habit of lumping foods into these categories as if an ingredient could be made entirely of just one of these fats (hence the tendency to treat saturated fats as a dietary devil, to be listed separately from all other fats on nutrition labels). But the truth is that all fats are a combination of these types of specific fats. Whatever type of fat happens to make up the majority of an oil or fat defines that oil or fat. While imprecise, this system is a handy way to organize different types of fat into overall categories, especially oils, which all contain 14 grams of fat per tablespoon. The differences lie in the proportions of fats they contain. Let's look at some common examples.

	Saturated Fat	Monounsaturated Fat	Polyunsaturated Fat
Olive oil	15 percent	70 percent	15 percent
Flax oil	15 percent	15 percent	70 percent
Coconut oil	85 percent	8 percent	7 percent

Given their proportions, it's fair to say that olive oil is a monounsaturated fat, flaxseed is a polyunsaturated fat and coconut is a saturated fat—yet in truth, they're combinations of all three. (Lard, by the way, is primarily a monounsaturated fat, albeit by a slim margin. If the lard is from pastured hogs, that margin gets wider.) But even though fats are all a combination of saturated and unsaturated fats, it's worth knowing the general category of whatever fat or oil you're using so that you know what kind of heat it can handle and therefore how you can best use it.

Now let's talk about how fats are built.

Understanding How Fats Are Built

How fats are built has everything to do with how they're best used in the kitchen and therefore how they affect our daily health. That's because of one simple reason: rancidity. We'll explore how processed oils become rancid in "How Oils Go Bad" (page 19), but for now, it's enough to know that saturated fats are more stable and therefore more resistant to heat and light (and time) than unsaturated fats are. In effect, saturated fats stay "fresh" longer. That freshness translates to improved nutritional benefits as well as better flavor.

It's time to take a brief tour of the structure of fats. First, let's clear up some potential confusion by defining terms. "Fats" and "oils" are both fats, structurally speaking. But like the terms "dough" and "batter," when people talk about fats and oils, they're generally using different words to describe different consistencies. We commonly say "fat" when we mean a fat that's solid at room temperature, and we say "oil" when we're talking about a fat that's liquid at room temperature. So in kitchen-speak, extra-virgin olive oil is an oil, while butter is a fat. (Just as batter is pourable and makes things like pancakes and muffins, whereas dough is thick enough to be shaped into things like cookies and loaves.)

When scientists talk about fats, they mean all fats regardless of consistency. It's like saying "baked goods" instead of splitting them into doughs and batters. In this chapter, when we talk about fats, we're referring to them the way scientists do, not the way cooks do.

Saturated and Unsaturated Fats

Both saturated and unsaturated fats are made of fatty acids that bond together in chains. How they form those bonds and what kinds of acids they are determines whether the final fat is saturated or unsaturated. Without getting into excessive details that might trigger flashbacks of high school chemistry classes, saturated fats are called "saturated" because they're joined directly to hydrogen atoms. They're *saturated* with hydrogen. Unsaturated fats contain double bonds rather than hydrogen, which is to say they're *unsaturated* by hydrogen, and they're not as cohesively connected. Monounsaturated fats have one double bond; polyunsaturated fats have more than one double bond. ("Poly" means "many.")

Whenever there's a double bond, there's more of a risk that a bond can be broken, and a broken bond is what leads to oxidation, or what a non-scientist would call rancidity or "going bad." (When you sniff milk, and it smells bad, you probably don't exclaim "Drat! The milk oxidized before I could drink it all!" You say, "The milk's gone bad!" It's the same thing.) Thus, polyunsaturated fats are by nature more prone to oxidizing than monounsaturated fats are, and saturated fats are the least likely to go bad because saturated fats don't have any double bonds. They're less fragile by nature, which means they're less susceptible to being damaged by heat and light.

Practical translation: If you leave unrefined flaxseed oil (which is primarily polyunsaturated), extra-virgin olive oil (mostly monounsaturated), and unrefined coconut oil (mostly saturated) in a sunny spot on your kitchen counter on a hot day, you'll kick-start rancidity in the flaxseed oil and not be doing any favors for the olive oil, but you won't bother the coconut oil. Saturated fats are simply more stable.

Trans Fats

Now you have a basic understanding of how fats are built and why they're sorted into saturated versus unsaturated categories. Before we move on to fine-print details, though, there is one more category of fats we need to address. It's one that's been hitting headlines for the past decade, ever since research started piling up that this fat is indisputably a bad idea: trans fats. Once heralded as a nutrition savior, trans fats are about to get the official boot from the U.S. Food and Drug Administration (FDA). Margarine is out; butter is back!

Trans fats are also called "hydrogenated" and "partially hydrogenated" oils. Other fats are being "interesterfied," which is a relatively new process but is often considered to be similar to hydrogenation. All of these fats are artificially created by using chemical catalysts to force hydrogen atoms between the double bonds of unsaturated fats. The resulting structure looks similar to a saturated fat and can function similarly in food production. That's why trans fats were originally made. They were a cheap substitute for butter, and they made it cheaper to manufacture any product normally made with butter.

Baked goods have long been a prime market for trans fats. If you make a cookie with an unsaturated fat (such as extra-virgin olive oil), the cookies will spread and flatten as they bake, and you'll wind up with a delicious thin crust of innumerable cookies joined together. If you make cookies with butter, coconut oil or trans fat, they remain separate disks. Of course, butter and coconut oil are more expensive than trans fats, so replacing butter with trans fats means bigger profits for mass-market food producers. Hence, trans fats have been a main ingredient in processed foods since the 1960s, despite research done since the 1950s indicating the damaging effect trans fats have on health. (Crisco, the first trans fat sold in the United States, debuted in 1911.)

Many restaurants, especially fast-food establishments, have historically fried their foods in trans fats. Considering that over half the meals Americans consume are eaten outside of the home, that's a lot of trans fat consumption. Trans fats have also been a popular ingredient in vegan, vegetarian, kosher and halal foods because trans fats are made of plant sources rather than animal sources. McDonald's used to cook its fries in beef tallow, for example, but switched to trans fats in response to consumers wanting to avoid animal products.

What's wrong with trans fats? Simply put, because they haven't been part of our food chain until very recently, our bodies don't know what to do with them. Because trans fats mimic saturated fats in structure, our bodies treat them as such and try to use them the way they'd use saturated fats—except that the artificially created trans fats can't perform the same functions. Instead, they interfere with cellular messaging, undermine our immune systems, kick-start heart disease and wreak general havoc on our normal body functions. Eating artificial trans fats is a very unhealthy idea.

That said, fat is never the black-and-white, good-and-bad issue that mainstream health authorities make it out to be. *Natural* trans fats do exist, and we've been consuming them ever since we've been eating ruminants like cows and sheep. These natural trans fats occur in the meat sourced from ruminants. One of these natural trans fats is called conjugated linoleic acid (CLA), and many studies have shown CLA to be beneficial to our health. (Not surprisingly, CLA doesn't have the same structure as artificially created trans fats have.) It might be a good idea to come up with an entirely different name for the natural trans fats to avoid confusion, but historically, artificial and natural trans fats have been lumped into one category. But the health is very much in the details! It's worth noting that the FDA ban on trans fats *only* refers to *artificial* trans fats, not natural trans fats such as CLA.

Want to avoid trans fats in your food? To determine whether a product contains harmful artificial trans fats, look for the words "hydrogenated," "partially hydrogenated" or "interesterified" on the ingredient label. If you see those ingredients listed, put that product back on the shelf.

How Oils Go Bad: Refinement and Rancidity

When it comes to oils—especially the quality of oils—it's not just how they're built (i.e., whether they're saturated, monounsaturated or polyunsaturated), it's how they're broken down. Broken-down or "refined" oils are oils that have been subjected to manufacturing processes that culminate in the oils being bleached and deodorized to mask the rancid appearance and smell of refined oils. After all, we can detect rancid foods, and we instinctively know we shouldn't eat them. Who hasn't whiffed a carton of milk to see if it's still good?

The easiest way to understand rancidity is to think about the "coleslaw scenario." Say it's summertime and you live in the Midwest. It's a typical hot and humid August day. You go to your favorite restaurant for lunch, order coleslaw and wind up taking some home. On your short drive home, you pop into the library to return a book, but after you walk in, you realize one of your favorite authors is doing a book signing. By the time you've bought a book, stood in line and gotten the author's autograph, it's an hour later. Are you still going to eat the coleslaw you left sitting on the front seat?

Hopefully not.

Now imagine it's a typical freezing Midwestern winter night. You had dinner at the same restaurant, left with the same coleslaw, drove home without turning on the heat and stopped by the library. Same scenario: You come out an hour later. Do you eat the coleslaw?

Sure. Why?

Let's look at what's different. In August at lunchtime, the hot, bright sun is high in the sky. On a winter night, it's cold and dark. Overheating something perishable such as coleslaw is a bad idea, and so is subjecting it to bright light. On a winter night though, your coleslaw is safe. Time is an element, too, because if you had gone straight home in August and popped the coleslaw into the fridge within ten minutes of putting it on the hot, bright car seat, it would have been fine. The coleslaw wouldn't have had time to go rancid. We know these things instinctively.

Another factor that causes rancidity is exposure to chemicals. Oxygen can negatively impact food; think of sliced apples and avocados. If you cover the exposed surface with plastic wrap and make sure no air gets to it, the slices won't brown. But when they are exposed to air, the surfaces will brown in as little as five minutes.

So we know what makes food go rancid: heat, light, time and chemicals. What most people don't realize is that refined oils are subjected to all of these factors. On the other hand, unrefined oils are quickly pressed under cool, dark conditions, and they are quickly bottled in opaque containers. Unrefined oils are not exposed to any rancidity-causing elements. Refined oils, on the other hand, are often heated to more than 500° Fahrenheit (260°C) and treated with a bevy of chemicals to leach every last droplet of oil from whatever ingredient is being processed (olives, sunflower seeds, canola seeds, etc.). No one cares about minimizing light exposure or making sure that these oils spend as little time as possible being refined.

By the time refined oils have made it to the end of the line, they're badly in need of bleaching and deodorizing. After all, who would buy a stinky, sludgy oil? Our natural instincts would warn us away from eating that product. That's why refined oils are odorless, tasteless and have the same bland golden color. They've been bleached and deodorized into neutral nothingness. Our ability to discern the rancidity of these oils has been neatly sidestepped.

Now that you know about refinement and rancidity, you've probably guessed that *unrefined*, high-quality oils have unique flavors, appearances and colors. You're right! Unrefined oils retain their original characteristics. In fact, one quick look and taste of an oil will probably be enough to clue you in on its refined/unrefined status.

Before we close this chapter, let's talk a little bit more about *why* we don't want to eat rancid foods. Our instincts tell us to throw away spoiled meat and rotten eggs, but why? There are solid reasons for our *yuck* reaction. Unlike a case of food poisoning—which hits hard but is usually gone in a day or so—the damage caused by rancid oils doesn't make itself quickly known. Rather, it's slow acting and longer term. Because that damage happens over the long term, it's hard to pin down exactly how rancid oil harms us. But most health experts agree that rancid oils aggravate/cause a host of chronic conditions, from cancer to neurological conditions to the group of diseases collectively known as "metabolic disorder" (diabetes, obesity, heart disease, etc.). No wonder we've developed an instinct to avoid rancid foods!

So let's embrace unrefined oils and drizzle/bake/sauté to our good health!

Omega 3s: What the Fuss Is All About and Where to Find Them

What do cold-water fish, flaxseeds and tender greens all have in common? They're all high in omega-3 fatty acids. So are walnuts, chia seeds and leafy herbs such as basil and mint. Omega-3 fats fall into the polyunsaturated fats category, and omega-3 fats in particular are anti-inflammatory. Considering that so many commonly consumed foods are inflammatory in nature—sugar and refined oils, to name just a few—from a health standpoint, it's important to balance the equation by enjoying foods rich in anti-inflammatory omega-3 fats.

We'll talk more about inflammatory foods in "Omega 6s: Too Much of a Good Thing" (page 22). In short, though, inflammation is a bad thing. Think of all the diseases ending in -itis, which refer to inflammatory conditions: colitis, tendonitis, arthritis, etc. Allergies and heart diseases such as atherosclerosis are also the result of inflammatory responses. In fact, most chronic diseases are linked to higher-than-normal levels of inflammation. Sometimes inflammation can be triggered by things we can't control (such as environmental factors like pollution, perfumes and eyes), but we *can* control whether or not we choose to eat inflammatory foods that will stoke the fires.

In the past, it wasn't difficult to find foods that were rich in anti-inflammatory omega-3 fats. Because these foods are so perishable, though, they don't have much of a place in today's processed-food sales model. Think of tender lettuce. How long can that sit on a shelf before it wilts and rots? A few days, perhaps. Ditto for basil and mint. Walnuts go rancid (read: taste bitter) faster than any other nut. On the flip side, foods heavy in inflammatory omega-6 fats have a longer lifespan. Safflower seeds outlast chia seeds; soy and corn oils outlast flaxseed and walnut oils. Processed foods that are mostly starch and sugar (with little or no omega-3 fats) can sit in a warehouse for months and emerge unchanged.

When you look at cuisines in cultures that rely on unprocessed, fresh foods, you'll find that omega-3 fats and omega-6 fats are eaten in equal amounts, or sometimes a 2:1 or 3:1 ratio in favor of omega-6s. In the processed food chain, however, the ratio is more like 20:1 in favor of omega-6 fats, or even as high as 50:1 depending on how much processed food a person eats. ("Processed food" also includes most restaurant meals, which again are dependent on sugar, refined oils, and starch- and sugar-based processed ingredients.) That's a pretty good recipe for winding up with inflammatory conditions and poor health.

So where can you find omega-3–rich foods? It helps to think about what being anti-inflammatory is. In the plant world, it means being flexible. Many parts of plants need to be sturdy and not so flexible—trunks, branches, roots, stems—so that the plant has structure and can support its own weight as it grows. The parts of a plant that typically need to be flexible, though, are the leaves. That's what's bendable. Hence leaves, such as lettuces, are a great source of omega-3 fats.

Blades of grass are bendable, too, but humans can't digest grass. We can, however, digest animal products from animals that *have* eaten grass (cows, sheep and goats) or that have eaten bugs that have eaten grass (chickens, ducks and turkeys). Whether you're talking about meat, eggs or dairy products, animals that have spent their lives nibbling on grass or critters that eat grass will yield products that are higher in omega-3 fats when compared with products from animals raised conventionally that are fed industrial products high in omega-6 fats.

Cold-water fish such as salmon and tuna are other great sources of omega-3 fats, as are smaller fish, including herring and sardines. That's because fish eat krill, which are tiny crustaceans that eat omega-3-rich algae and other marine plants. Larger fish eat the smaller fish that have eaten the krill. Once again, it's an up-the-food-chain situation. Farmed fish that don't have access to krill or krill-eating fish won't be as rich in omega-3 fats.

Fish in general contain higher amounts of omega-3 fats than land animals. Why? If you're a weight-bearing land animal that has to be able to stand up against gravity, you need a more structured, less flexible body than if you're a floating, water-dwelling fish. So in general, fish and foods from the sea contain higher levels of omega-3 fats than foods from the land. Also, seaweed and sea vegetables are particularly rich sources of omega-3 fats.

Aside from bendable parts of plants (tender lettuces, leafy herbs and grape leaves), pastured animal products, and foods from the sea (including roe), there are a handful of other foods rich in omega-3 fats, such as walnuts, flaxseeds and chia seeds. Just be sure to keep the seeds and nuts—and the oils made from those seeds and nuts!—in the refrigerator so they don't go rancid, and don't heat the oils, which would destroy them. Also remember that an unprocessed food rich in omega-3 fats is a better option than a processed food that has omega-3 fats artificially added to it. Processed sources of omega-3s are more faded than fresh sources. They're especially prone to going rancid because they're more delicate to begin with. A bottle of refrigerated flaxseed oil is more protected than, say, granola that has been tossed in flaxseed oil and then bagged in clear packaging and not refrigerated.

Once you know what to look for, it isn't difficult to find foods rich in omega-3 fats, and it's a snap to serve them in various ways. How about a salad made with leaf lettuce, walnuts and blue cheese from grass-fed cows? Toss it with some flaxseed oil and hard-boiled eggs from pastured hens, and you have an impressively anti-inflammatory meal. Or how about wild salmon filets served with a generous dollop of pesto? Make homemade ice cream with cream from grass-fed cows and eggs from pastured hens and drizzle it with walnut oil for a nutty finish. Sprinkle on some chia seeds, too. They'll provide a nice crunch and a gorgeous visual effect.

So now you know: Omega-3 fats are healthy, and they're delicious, too.

Sources of Omega-3 Fats

- Leaves: lettuces, mixed greens, dandelion greens, grape leaves, celery leaves and large-leafed herbs such as basil and mint

- Cold-water fish: salmon and tuna

- Small, krill-eating fish: sardines, herring, anchovies and smelt

- Wild-caught seafood in general

- Fish eggs

- Crustaceans: crab, shrimp, lobster and crayfish

- Seaweed and sea vegetables: dulse, nori, kombu, wakame, hijiki, kelp, sea palm and samphire

- Eggs, meat, and dairy products from pastured and wild animals

- Certain seeds and nuts and their oils: flaxseeds, chia seeds, radish seeds and walnuts

Omega 6s: Too Much of a Good Thing

If you've ever had sore muscles or a swollen throat, you know that being inflamed is uncomfortable and at times downright painful. Then again, inflammation is a sign that your body's immune system is kicking in to wipe out a virus, heal an injury or destroy bacteria. When you get a cut and the skin at the edge of the cut gets puffy, for example, inflammation helps to seal the cut and start the recovery process. If the blood didn't clot, a relatively slight injury could be fatal. Yet it's inflammatory responses that cut down on the blood's natural anticoagulant properties to allow that clotting to happen. So we need a certain amount of inflammation to maintain good health.

The problem, though, is that most people living in Western nations are inflamed on a daily basis, thanks to their reliance on processed, inflammatory foods, along with increased levels of stress, not enough sound sleep and not enough exercise. Living in a constant state of over-reactive inflammation undermines our immune systems. They're too busy responding inappropriately to be able to perform their proper defensive functions.

Over-reactive inflammation makes us susceptible to opportunistic bacteria, viruses and even cancers. In other words, being inflamed makes us more likely to get sick.

The mainstays of modern food systems are less-perishable products, which in turn are based on ingredients high in sugars, starches and inflammatory omega-6 fats. These ingredients are shelf-stable, and they represent higher profit margins for manufacturers and grocers because such products are less likely to spoil and have to be thrown out. Consumers view these less-perishable goods as a "deal" because they seemingly last forever. (Note that some long-lasting products *are* a great idea in terms of flavor and nutrition, including frozen produce and meats, canned produce and seafood, and dried products such as whole grains and beans. But these items require a little bit of preparation, and they are often passed over in favor of instant open-the-bag-and-eat gratification.)

Foods high in inflammatory omega-6 fats include safflower, grape seed, sunflower and cottonseed oils, which are some of the most common "vegetable oils" used in processed foods, restaurants and the kitchens of unwitting home cooks. Soy and corn—which are the staples of nearly every processed food, from crackers and chips to cereals and baked goods—are high in omega-6 fats. Shortenings, spreads and margarines are also based on those omega-6-heavy ingredients. Wheat is high in omega-6 fats, and wheat is in the majority of processed foods in some form.

Meat, eggs and dairy products from animals raised conventionally and fed diets based on processed corn, soy and refined oil products are high in inflammatory omega-6 fats, as opposed to meat, eggs and dairy products from animals grazing/feeding in their natural outdoor habitats. These animals eat grass, plants and bugs that are high in anti-inflammatory omega-3 fats. Farmed fish tend to be higher in omega-6 fats than wild-caught fish because like conventional livestock, farmed fish are often fed ingredients that are high in omega-6 fats. It's worth paying more for wild salmon. It tastes better, too!

Fortunately, once you veer away from processed foods and start relying on fresh ingredients you prepare yourself, it's easy to ditch inflammatory omega-6-rich foods and focus on anti-inflammatory omega-3-rich foods instead. And it's much more delicious, too. Why settle for a flavorless refined vegetable oil when you can enjoy rich, nutty, unrefined walnut oil? Scrap rubbery processed cheese in favor of intensely savory cheese from grass-fed animals. I bet you'll enjoy flavorful, moist chicken thighs from pastured chickens a lot more than dry conventional breasts that taste like cardboard. Have you ever grown your own herbs or lettuce? All you need is a pot and a sunny windowsill.

Sources of Omega-6 Fats

- Most seeds and their oils: safflower seeds, sunflower seeds, grape seeds and cotton seeds

- Soy and products made with soy

- Corn and products made with corn

- Wheat and products made with wheat

- Shortenings, spreads, margarines and other butter substitute foods

- Farmed fish and seafood is higher in omega-6 fats than wild-caught fish and seafood

- Eggs, meat and dairy products from animals raised conventionally are higher in omega-6 fats than products from pastured and wild animals

- Processed foods are generally high in inflammatory omega-6 fats

Saturated Fats: Stable and Sturdy Standbys

If you've ever cooked with ghee, you've witnessed the stability of saturated fat in action. Rather than turning into burnt smoke as it hits its smoke point or catching on fire as it hits its flash point (that's how grease fires happen), ghee simply melts and sits placidly in its skillet, even when that skillet is on high heat. That's because ghee has a smoke point of nearly 500°F (260°C). Why? Because more than 60 percent of the fat in ghee is saturated, and saturated fats are inherently more stable than unsaturated fats. (See "Understanding How Fats Are Built" on page 16 for more details.) Other saturated fats include butter, coconut oil, red palm oil and palm kernel oil. Ghee, though, contains the highest levels of saturated fats, and it can therefore handle the highest level of heat.

The ability to handle higher levels of heat is exactly what makes saturated fats so useful. Decreased susceptibility to heat and light means that saturated fats are naturally more shelf-stable than unsaturated fats and oils, too, so saturated fats can be stored at room temperature for longer periods of time. Coconut oil and palm kernel oil are ideally suited for use in tropical environments because they can be stored at hotter temperatures for longer periods of time without going rancid. Ghee is ideal for people living in the hot Indian subcontinent because ghee doesn't need to be refrigerated. (In North Africa and the Middle East, ghee is purposely fermented, sometimes for years, and it is a highly valued cooking ingredient.)

Even if you don't live in a hot region, saturated fats are useful when cooking over high heat, such as with wok cooking or deep-frying. Deep-frying, by the way, doesn't have to be done in a deep vat of oil. You can melt a knob of ghee in a small skillet to coat the bottom, then "deep-fry" fritters, flatbreads or thinly sliced veggies. Saturated fats are also great to use when you're roasting or grilling at higher temperatures.

But what about the decades-old idea that saturated fats are harmful? While research into that contentious subject continues, it's worth noting that the initial research on saturated fats done in the 1950s and '60s was conducted well before the harmful effects of *trans fats* were known. During the course of those now hotly contested experiments, saturated fats were lumped together with trans fats, and they were therefore assumed to be just as damaging.

One of the prominent researchers of the era, Dr. Ancel Keys, conducted a famous study wherein he surveyed a range of countries and published his famous Seven Countries Study, showing the correlation between improved health and lower amounts of ingested dietary fat, particularly saturated fat. Critics, however, point out that Dr. Keys handpicked the countries that supported his original anti-saturated-fat hypothesis and that in fact the vast majority—nearly two-thirds—of the countries he studied did *not* support his conclusions.

Also, as many critics have also pointed out, Dr. Keys did not take into account the differing amounts of sugar consumed in the countries he studied. Sugar is proving itself to be tightly linked to chronic diseases such as diabetes, heart disease and even cancer. The countries Dr. Keys said were the most healthy because of low fat intake were also countries where people's consumption of sugar was low. More and more studies (both new ongoing studies and reevaluation of older studies like Dr. Keys' Seven Countries Study) are showing that the populations with the lowest sugar consumption show the lowest incidences of chronic disease. Fat—especially saturated fat—may have just been in the wrong place at the wrong time.

Since the 1950s, the "eat fat, get fat" idea was also embraced by the sugar industry, which was looking for ways to boost its sales in the wake of post–World War II rationing. During wartime, Americans had gotten used to making due with less sugar because rationing was strictly enforced from 1942 to 1947. Marketing executives came up with advertising campaigns designed to get sugar back in cupboards and on tables, such as ads in women's magazines that compared a spoonful of white sugar with an apple and told their readers that the sugar was preferable because it contained fewer calories. No one would agree with this today.

In retrospect, it seems obvious that sugar industry leaders embraced the "eat fat, get fat" mantra as a way to divert public attention away from the potential downfalls of sugar consumption, which was starting to become more and more apparent by that time, especially in light of the research being done on diabetes. After all, until the 1930s, type 2 diabetes was so rare that most doctors referred to it as "hyperinsulinism," not diabetes. The word "diabetes" meant what we now refer to as type 1 diabetes. After sugar consumption skyrocketed, incidences of type 2 diabetes rose, and now type 2 cases account for more than 90 percent of diabetes in the United States. The blame for diabetes and many other chronic conditions is finally shifting away from fat and toward sugar.

Now that many people are shedding the anti-fat dogma that took hold in the 1950s and '60s, it's getting easier to find long-lasting, heat-tolerant saturated fats such as ghee, butter and tropical oils. It's time to restock the pantry!

Cholesterol: An Overlooked Nutrient

Cholesterol has been a hotly debated topic since the late 1950s, when Dr. Keys published his Seven Countries Study. In addition to showing a correlation between improved health and lower amounts of ingested dietary fat, the study also linked saturated fats and cholesterol with heart disease. Since then, other researchers have pointed out that Dr. Keys' results only held true for seven out of the twenty-one countries he studied. Also, he didn't take sugar intake into consideration, which also sheds considerable doubt on his results in light of more recent research pointing to the many deleterious effects of sugar consumption. But Dr. Keys' study became a battle cry for governmental agencies and medical authorities. That was when butter got the boot, and margarine was heralded as a health food. Now, of course, the heavily refined trans fats contained in margarine are known to be such a health hazard that the U.S. Food and Drug Administration is considering a ban on artificially produced trans fats, and many diners are ditching margarine in favor of cholesterol-containing butter. (Note that Dr. Keys' study also did not consider the effects of trans fats or rancid fats.)

So is cholesterol good or bad? Some researchers staunchly cling to the ideas presented in the Seven Countries Study and say that we should limit our consumption of cholesterol. Other researchers say that because our bodies need cholesterol, if we don't eat enough of it, our bodies simply produce more. In other words, they believe that our serum (blood) levels are not a reflection of the cholesterol we eat. Some researchers say that cholesterol is an antioxidant and therefore has protective properties. Many large studies (such as the Framingham Heart Study and Vorarlberg Health Monitoring and Prevention Programme) have found that the risk for having a heart attack *increases* when people have *low* cholesterol levels. Even mainstream medical sources say that only half of heart-attack patients have high cholesterol. Half. The other half of heart-attack patients have low cholesterol. A fifty-fifty shot doesn't say much in terms of causality. And the definition of "high" and "low" cholesterol levels—as well as the type of cholesterol thought to be problematic—varies from decade to decade. Again, that's hardly definitive.

What we can say about cholesterol is that all animals need it, which is why animal products always contain cholesterol. Cholesterol is a crucial part of the membrane of every cell in our bodies. It provides enough of a structure to keep what's inside the cells from leaking out, yet cholesterol lends the membranes enough fluidity to allow messages to flow into and out of the cells. In other words, it's the backbone of the communications infrastructure, and common sense tells us that chaos ensues when communications break down. Think about what happens when the IT department is out to lunch and the internet connections cut out, the phone lines go down, the printers go off-line, etc. Everything falls apart. Likewise, when cellular signaling and intracellular transport can't occur, our internal systems can't function properly. Then we're far more likely to wind up sick, sometimes seriously so.

What else does cholesterol have to offer? We also need it to synthesize vitamin D, and Americans are often told they lack sufficient levels of vitamin D. In the liver, cholesterol becomes bile, which contains bile salts. We need bile salts to digest fats and fat-soluble vitamins A, D, E and K. We also need cholesterol to manufacture steroid hormones, several of which are sex hormones that are involved with fertility (i.e., estrogen and androgen). Cholesterol also seems to play a role in brain function. Low levels of cholesterol are linked to depression and other mental disorders.

In terms of figuring out if a food contains cholesterol or not, it's pretty easy: Is it a plant? Plants don't contain cholesterol, whereas all animals need cholesterol to function. So meat, eggs, dairy products, seafood and fish—all non-plants—contain cholesterol. Nuts, seeds, vegetables, fruits and grains—all plants—do not contain cholesterol. It's not complicated. A bag of frozen corn screaming the words "Zero cholesterol!" is stating the obvious. Because cholesterol is present in animal foods, cholesterol-containing foods are also high in protein and fat and low in carbohydrates and sugars. (Milk is the sugariest of the lot because it contains lactose, which is a sugar. Anything ending in –ose is a sugar.)

So, should you eat cholesterol or no cholesterol? Considering how vital cholesterol is to all animals, it's not surprising that the decades-old advice to eat egg whites and not the cholesterol-containing yolks is falling by the wayside. It might just be time for a paradigm shift.

Oils in the Kitchen

Finding unrefined oils can be tricky, because often the only true tests are flavor and aroma. An unrefined oil tastes and smells like what it is, while refined oils have virtually zero flavor and zero aroma, although some are so refined that their rancid taste is noticeable. Refined oils are also all the same neutral color, whereas unrefined oils retain their pigments. If you look at a bottle of refined peanut oil next to a bottle of unrefined peanut oil, you'll notice that the refined oil is the same pale golden color as vegetable oil, canola oil, grape seed oil and every other refined oil on the shelf. The unrefined peanut oil, on the other hand, has a rich mahogany color that will remind you of…guess what? Peanuts!

Of course, when you're at the grocery store, you can't just start opening bottles of oil to sniff and taste them. Specialty-goods stores, however, may have a "you're welcome to taste" policy, and if you ask, they may give you samples. For example, visitors to Zingerman's Deli in Ann Arbor, Michigan, are exhorted to try everything in the larder, from butternut squash oil to innumerable varieties of extra-virgin olive oils. Shops dedicated to extra-virgin olive oils often offer tastings to anyone who walks in. Perhaps you have a friend with a few unrefined oils in the pantry who'd like to host an impromptu oil tasting.

Once you've tried an oil and found it to be a flavorful unrefined oil, look for more oils from that same producer. Whenever possible, do a little on-the-spot research. Look up the product and the company that makes it to see how the oil is produced, or ask employees for their opinion of the oil and what it tastes like. Better yet, take this book with you to the store as a reference. Even if you don't have any information at hand, you can look at the way the oil is packaged and the terms on the label to help determine if you're looking at an unrefined, high-quality oil.

Oil Packaging

Start with the bottle. Is it made of flimsy plastic or opaque glass? You'll notice that vegetable oil, which is arguably the most-refined, lowest-quality oil on the shelf, is packaged in thin, see-through plastic. Light and heat are constantly affecting that oil. A bottle of extra-virgin olive oil, on the other hand, is probably in a dark-green glass bottle, shielded from light and heat thanks to the glass. A bottle of unrefined walnut oil might even be in a completely opaque bottle that blocks all light. Flaxseed oil is often stored in opaque glass bottles in a refrigerated case at the store. Unrefined coconut oil, though, is likely in a clear glass jar. That's because it's a saturated fat and therefore far more shelf-stable than its unsaturated cousins.

Remember the factors that make oil go rancid: light, heat, time and chemicals. High-quality oils are packaged in ways that mitigate light and heat, and they often bear "bottled on" date stamps so that you know how long they've been sitting around. Also unrefined oils are processed without chemicals. In contrast, refined oils have already been rendered rancid and then have been degummed, deodorized and chemically bleached to make them odorless, flavorless and, to the uninformed consumer, seemingly "good forever." The truth is, these oils expired when they were refined.

In this case, appearances *do* mean a lot: please judge the oil by its bottle!

Useful Terms

Beyond judging bottle quality, you can read labels to find out more about an oil's unrefined/refined state. Here's where we get to the tricky part, though. Most of these terms are not regulated, and even the big one we're all familiar with doesn't mean as much as we think it means. We'll start with that one.

Extra-Virgin

This designation means that the olive oil is of the highest possible quality: It must have been pressed and then bottled quickly under cold conditions from undamaged olives at the peak of their ripeness. The only process it may have undergone was filtering. (Note that when olive oil is refrigerated, it takes on a half-liquid, half-solid texture and looks murky. The white "floaties" that you may see collecting at the bottom of the bottle are drops of solidified oil, not flakes of olive flesh. This has nothing to do with filtering or lack thereof; this is simply what happens when a monounsaturated fat is chilled.) The free acidity of the finished oil cannot exceed 0.8 percent, which means the oil will have a pleasant, fresh flavor.

Because extra-virgin olive oil tastes like the olive it was pressed from and because there are many varieties of olives, each extra-virgin olive oil has a unique flavor. That's why it's best to visit a shop specializing in oils, especially extra-virgin olive oil. Then you can taste each variety to see which one you like best. It's also a great way to develop a taste for unrefined oils. Once you start upgrading to flavorful, high-quality oils, you'll quickly be able to taste the difference between high-quality oils and low-quality oils, thus making it easier to avoid the latter.

Note that the official "extra-virgin" designation only applies to olive oil. Other oils may state "extra-virgin" on their labels, but they aren't regulated the same way. And unfortunately, investigations by global olive oil authorities, many of them based in Mediterranean olive-producing regions such as Spain, Italy and Greece, and research universities such as University of California (UC) Davis are finding that olive oil producers may be fudging the term "extra-virgin."

In an April 2011 study, the UC Davis Olive Center tested the free acidity levels of a variety of top-selling oils to determine which oils truly adhered to the extra-virgin regulations. The result? Only two out of eight brands passed the test. The others failed to meet the standards. Olive oils produced by California Olive Ranch and Cobram Estate passed with flying colors, while 56 percent of the Colavita samples didn't pass the free-acidity tests. It got worse: 61 percent of the Star "extra-virgin" olive oil didn't pass, 72 percent of Bertolli's samples didn't pass, 83 percent of Filippo Berio didn't pass, and a whopping 94 percent of Pompeian didn't pass. The takeaway here? Just because an olive oil bottle says "extra-virgin" doesn't mean that it is. (Report: Evaluation of Extra-Virgin Olive Oil Sold in California, UC Davis Olive Center, olivecenter.ucdavis.edu, April 2011.)

Virgin Oil

You'll mostly see this designation on olive oil, but it's also common to see it on coconut oil. Virgin olive oil is made from lesser-quality olives, such as the bruised and blemished ones that have fallen to the ground—as opposed to the ripe olives still hanging on the branches. The production process is similar to extra-virgin oil production, but the free acidity can range up to 1.5 percent. That higher number represents a loss of flavor as well as a loss of beneficial antioxidants. Often, virgin oils masquerade as extra-virgin because producers know people are willing to pay a higher price, which is justified if the oil really *is* extra-virgin, for oil bearing that label. Overall quality standards are not as stringent for virgin olive oil as they are for extra-virgin olive oil.

Not many studies have been done on non-olive oils that bear this designation, so when it comes to non-olive "virgin" oils, you'll have to rely on your taste buds and nose to determine how unrefined and authentic the oil in question is.

Pomace Oil

You may have seen a gallon-size metal jerry can of pomace oil on sale for $4.99 and thought, "What a deal!" It's not. If pomace oil were alcohol, it would be classified as "rotgut." This is the most refined kind of olive oil on the market, and unfortunately it's often just called "olive oil" and nobody is the wiser, except, of course, for people who regularly enjoy extra-virgin olive oil and can taste a pretender as soon as the oil makes tongue contact.

Pomace is made from the waste left over from virgin and extra-virgin olive oil production: the pits, skins, stems, etc. Because very little oil remains in the debris, the only way to extract this oil is through the heavy refinement methods described in "How Oils Go Bad" (page 19). As Tom Mueller describes this oil in *Extra Virginity*, his landmark book about the olive oil industry published in 2011, pomace oil comes off the manufacturing line in a sorry state: "What's left is a dense, black liquid known as crude pomace oil...before this oil can be sold as food, it's piped into a refinery in an adjoining building for desolventization, deacidification, deodorization, degumming, and other chemical processes."

Mueller goes on to point out that European authorities have found traces of carcinogenic and toxic substances in pomace oil, but unwary shoppers and diners continue to unwittingly consume pomace oil in everything from innocuous-sounding bottles of "olive oil" to many meals eaten in restaurants. "Pomace oil is used extensively in the food service industry and in many restaurants," Mueller points out, "as well as an ingredient in foods such as pizza, pasta sauces, and snack foods." If you're an avid label-reader, you've certainly noticed "olive oil" listed as an ingredient on countless products. It's probably pomace oil.

And it isn't just in prepared foods. Pomace oil lurks in the oils section more than you'd think. No law prevents it from being labeled simply as "olive oil." Often, pomace is blended with virgin oil, slapped with the word "healthy," and sold as olive oil. It's hard to tell the difference, especially if you haven't experienced the full, rich flavor of 100 percent extra-virgin olive oil. You probably haven't noticed the flat, off-tasting flavor of pomace oil when it's blended into sauces and used in snack foods. Once you've upgraded your oils, though, you'll soon perceive that refined/rancid flavor.

Refined Oil

Unlike the terms we've talked about relating to olive oil, "refined" doesn't apply specifically to olives, and it's a generic term with no regulated meaning. Typically, though, oils that are marked "refined" have undergone a process similar to what pomace oil has undergone. 'Nuff said. It's also worth noting that vegetable oil is a refined oil. It's called "vegetable" because it can be made of whatever commodity crop is cheapest—corn, soy, cottonseed, canola, etc.—without the manufacturer having to change the label. Does your window squeak when you push it up? If you don't have any WD-40 on hand, rub the frame with vegetable oil. It's a great household lubricant. Just don't pour it on your salad.

Unrefined Oil

Again, this is an unregulated term, although when an oil has flavor, aroma, unique color and absolutely tastes like what it's made from, it's an unrefined oil. Sometimes you may see the word "unrefined" on a label; other times you won't. Some oil producers sell both refined and unrefined versions of an oil. Spectrum, for example, produces refined and unrefined peanut oil. The former has no aroma and no flavor; the latter is so powerfully peanutty that upon opening it, you'll hope that nobody with a peanut allergy is within 50 feet (15 m) of you!

Many unrefined oils also state their upper heat limit clearly on the label. After all, the oil producers have created a high-quality product that is being sold at a higher price, and they don't want you to inadvertently overheat your oil, thus causing it to become prematurely rancid and possibly even start a smoke or grease fire. Seeing an upper temperature listed on an oil bottle is a good sign that the oil is unrefined. The upper heat limit of extra-virgin olive oil is around 325°F (160°C), for example, while unrefined peanut oil is good up to 395°F (200°C). That's because peanut oil has slightly more monounsaturated fat and slightly less polyunsaturated fat than olive oil does, which makes peanut oil less sensitive to heat. So it's worth looking for stated upper-limit temperatures on labels. Just know that sometimes refined oils also have stated temperatures, so that's not an absolute guarantee.

Cold-Pressed/Expeller-Pressed Oil

This is a confusing term that lacks official regulation. Unrefined oils *are* created by cold-pressing the original nut/seed/fruit, and they *are* mechanically expeller-pressed rather than being treated with chemical solvents. But the definition of what kind of machinery constitutes "expeller-pressed" is up for grabs, and even if an oil has been cold-pressed originally, it may go on to be superheated and refined much the same way pomace and other refined oils are.

If you've gone from avid label reading to savvy label reading, you've probably noticed that cold-pressed/expeller-pressed oils tend to be listed as an ingredient in processed foods such as chips and puffed green "peas" that are made of compressed pea starch, binders and cold-pressed canola or grape seed oil. Not nearly as much research has been done on cold-pressed and expeller-pressed oils compared with the various grades of olive oil, but the way these oils are used as ingredients suggests that the majority of them are refined.

Natural Oil, Pure Oil, Extra Light Oil, Light Oil, Light-Tasting Oil, Extra Light-Tasting Oil

None of these terms mean anything, although it's a safe bet that if the manufacturer is trying to woo you with healthy-sounding words, that oil has been refined to the hilt.

Storing Oils and Fats: Protecting Your Investment

Once you understand what makes oils and fats go rancid (see "How Oils Go Bad" on page 19), you have a pretty good idea of how to *not* make them go rancid: Don't expose them to heat, light or air, and don't plan on keeping them around indefinitely. That said, it's best to look at each of those scenarios more closely. We'll also take a look at how each kind of fat (saturated, monounsaturated and polyunsaturated) is affected by those rancidity-causing factors.

Heat and Light

Don't keep your oils or fats by any sources of heat. Those include stoves, ovens, toaster ovens or any other appliance that generates heat. Sources of light also usually generate heat, too, so keep your oils and fats in cool, dark places. (There's a reason the refrigerator is completely dark when the door is closed!) Even non-heat-emitting light sources will cause oils and fats to degrade more quickly. That's why high-quality oils are typically packaged in opaque or semi-opaque containers.

Some worst-case storage scenarios? Next to the stove and/or on the windowsill. Yes, it's convenient to keep oil by the stove, and it's pretty to keep it on the windowsill, but the convenience/aesthetic factor is *not* worth the damage done to the oil and consequently to yourself. Always think "cool and dark," such as a cupboard that is not next to or directly above a stove or any other source of heat. Or better yet, stash your oils and fats in the fridge. That's the best place for them. Then your investment will be well protected.

Air and Time

Just as metal rusts when exposed to air, oils and fats go rancid when exposed to air. That means it's imperative to keep your oils and fats in tightly closed containers—not in cute little pitchers with pour spouts! Your best bet is to leave your oils in their original containers and keep them tightly closed.

Time matters, too, when it comes to oils and fats. Because saturated fats are the most stable, the more saturated a fat is, the longer you can keep it around, even when stored at room temperature. But monounsaturated fats should be refrigerated for no longer than six months (or perhaps a year if the oil is very, very fresh), and polyunsaturated oils are best consumed within three months.

You should also always refrigerate polyunsaturated oils. You might want to write the purchase date on your oils so that you have a ballpark estimate of how long they've been in your refrigerator/cool and dark pantry. Many high-quality oils are also stamped with the date they were pressed.

How to Know If You've Stored Your Oils Properly

The best way to determine whether or not your oil is fresh is to pay attention to how it tastes and smells. Rancid oils start tasting bitter and extremely oily, and the more rancid they become, the more off-putting their scent is. You'll develop a sensitivity to rancidity once you switch from already-rancid conventional oils to flavorful, unrefined oils. It doesn't take long to be able to taste the difference between fresh and rancid oil.

Storing Saturated Fats

Because saturated fats are the most stable fats, they can best withstand the effects of heat, light, air and time. You can store saturated fats at room temperature, although again, it's best to keep them in a cool and dark place. Some fats that are primarily saturated will liquefy when they reach 78°F (25°C) or so, but they'll still be fine. When the ambient temperature drops below 78°F (25°C), they'll re-solidify. Coconut oil in particular reacts that way.

People often store ghee and butter in the fridge, which is absolutely fine to do. It'll lengthen their life. And sometimes it's good to have chilled, rock-hard butter, such as when you're making pie crusts and streusels. Then again, sometimes you want softer butter, for example when you want to cream it for baking recipes. Just let the butter sit at room temperature for about ten minutes. (That's only true for butter made with cream from pastured cows. Conventional butter takes an hour to soften because it contains more saturated fat thanks to the fact that the cows are improperly fed and not allowed to exercise.) But ultimately, the decision is yours, because saturated fats can be stored either at room temperature or in the refrigerator.

Storing Monounsaturated Oils

Monounsaturated oils are liquid at room temperature and semi-liquid when refrigerated. They're less stable than saturated fats, so you have to be more aware of how you treat monounsaturated oils. If you're going to rip through your extra-virgin olive oil in three months, it's fine to keep it in a dark, cool place. Then it'll be easier to pour, as opposed to being refrigerated and a semi-liquid. But if you aren't going to use your monounsaturated oils within three months, refrigerate them.

Storing Polyunsaturated Oils

When it comes to polyunsaturated oils, the rule is simple: Always refrigerate them. These are very fragile oils, and they need to be chilled to prolong their life. Flaxseed oil, walnut oil, sesame seed oil, pumpkin seed oil, butternut squash seed oil and hemp seed oil are all polyunsaturated oils and absolutely must be refrigerated at all times to maintain maximum freshness. You'll notice that they're polyunsaturated because they'll be free-flowing liquid straight out of the refrigerator. (In contrast to monounsaturated oils, which are semi-liquid once refrigerated, and saturated fats, which are solid when chilled.) Don't cook with polyunsaturated oils, either. They'll easily scorch and turn rancid. You can, however, drizzle polyunsaturated oils over just-cooked dishes as a delicious garnish. (Or use them in chilled/not-heated dishes.)

A final note about polyunsaturated oils: Walnut and flaxseed oils are high in anti-inflammatory omega-3 fats, which are highly beneficial. (And also highly perishable.) Use these flavorful and healthful oils whenever you get the chance!

Flavor Families and Culinary Uses: Choosing the Best Oil for the Job

Now that you're an expert on unrefined oils, it's time to have fun with them! The first consideration when choosing a particular oil for a particular dish is heat tolerance. If you wanted to keep things as simple as possible, you could just have ghee and extra-virgin olive oil in your pantry. Use ghee whenever you want to cook at high heat, and use olive oil for everything else, including baking. If you're a big fan of roasted vegetables, you might also want to have a jar of coconut oil on hand because it'll easily handle the 375°F–400°F (190°C–205°C) temperature you'd use when roasting. But you really don't need any more variety than those.

If you've read this far, though, I bet you'd like to explore the deliciously nutritious world of unrefined oils. They're a joy to use in everyday dishes, they're fun to showcase during an oil-tasting party, and they're ideal ingredients to dress up any dinner when you want to impress your guests. And if you refrigerate them, nearly all oils have a long shelf life. You can even freeze them if you happen to collect a few too many.

So let's talk flavor. Aside from the predominant flavor of oils, it's also useful to know where they're originally from and which cuisines feature them. You'll never run out of ways to enjoy your unrefined, full-flavored oils.

To make it easier to ponder the possibilities offered by flavor-forward unrefined oils, I've classified them as one of five types: nuts, fruits, seeds, tropicals or animal fats. You can use them any way you'd like, of course—as long as you pay attention to their heat tolerance—but it's worth noting a few characteristics that they have in common.

Nut Oils

Some nut oils are powerfully nutty; others are a bit more modest. Even the seriously nutty nut oils, though, fade in flavor when heated. That can be a good thing if don't want your roasted veggies to taste peanutty. But in some dishes, you might prefer to have more of a nutty finish. If you do want to bring out the nut flavor, use the nut oil as a finishing drizzle, even if you've also cooked the dish with it. Just remember not to heat walnut oil! (It is a polyunsaturated oil and so falls into the category of "don't heat them" oils.) Be sure to store walnut oil in the fridge because it is very sensitive to heat.

Fruit Oils

Fruit oils aren't as plentiful as nut oils, but both of them—olive and avocado—are endlessly versatile. They both handle medium heat, so you can sauté with them, and they both fit well with Mediterranean-inspired dishes.

Just like avocados, avocado oil is mild, with a faintly sweet flavor and hint of creaminess. You can pair avocado oil with anything.

Extra-virgin olive oils vary greatly in terms of flavor: Some are spicy and throat-biting, others are buttery and still others are grassy and bright. Always taste your olive oil before deciding how to use it. Smooth-tasting varieties are great in baked goods (swap out that vegetable oil for extra-virgin olive oil), while spicier, more flavorful olive oils are great in dressings and sautés.

Seed Oils

Due to seed oils' higher proportions of polyunsaturated fat, they don't do well with heat. Be sure to store them in the fridge.

Seed oils are very flavorful, and they work beautifully in non-heated dishes, especially as finishing drizzles. Most people don't realize how many opportunities there are to use these unique oils, several of which offer high levels of anti-inflammatory omega-3 fats. Here is a list of suggestions.

• Blend oils into cold dips or add spices and herbs directly to oils and serve them as a dipping/drizzling oil.

• Make your own dressings by whisking vinegar or citrus juice with oil and perhaps some herbs or Dijon mustard.

• Drizzle oils onto cooked dishes just before serving.

• Soft cheeses such as mozzarella and goat cheese logs are lovely when drizzled with flavorful oils.

• Drizzle onto ice cream and other desserts as a flavorful finishing touch.

• Add oils to smoothies. (Remember, most vitamins are fat-soluble, so fruit- and veggie-based smoothies benefit greatly from the presence of unrefined oils and fats.)

• Stir oils into cooked grains/seeds and mashed roots.

• Toss cooked or raw veggies with oils.

• Garnish fresh fruit with a drizzle of oil.

Tropical Oils

Only three oils fall into this category: coconut, palm and palm kernel oil. One of them—coconut oil—has snagged the spotlight. Coconut oil is milder in flavor than palm oil, plus it's more shelf-stable because it's higher in saturated fat. The beauty of coconut oil being mostly saturated fat is that it can handle medium-high heat, which is an ability not too many oils share. It's also solid at room temperature and doesn't need to be refrigerated.

Palm oil and palm kernel oil come from the same fruit, but they're quite different in appearance and usage. Unrefined palm oil is primarily a monounsaturated fat, not a saturated fat, so it's suited for medium rather than high heat. It comes from the palm fruit itself, whereas palm kernel oil is pressed from the kernel of the fruit. Palm oil's earthy flavor is very distinct and not as easy to pair with dishes as the milder-tasting palm kernel oil is. Also, palm oil is a striking bright red that will stain the finished dish red, much like paprika does. But that bright red represents the world's best source of vitamin A, especially because those gorgeous beta-carotene pigments come pre-packaged with the fat your body needs to make use of them. Plus, if you want to make truly authentic Brazilian or Malaysian cuisine, break out the palm oil! Many African cuisines also take advantage of palm oil's full flavor and beautiful color.

Palm kernel oil, on the other hand, is nearly as saturated as coconut oil, so it's ideal for higher-heat cooking. And its off-white color won't be seen in your finished dish. Both palm kernel oil and red palm oil can be tricky to find, though. Coconut oil is far more readily available. Also, because most palm oil is not produced using sustainable practices, many people choose to avoid palm oils for environmental reasons. That constantly shifting political issue is outside of the scope of this book; you'll have to decide if it's a factor for you.

Animal Fats

Any rendered animal fat can be used for cooking: lard or bacon drippings from pigs, schmaltz from goose or ducks or chickens, tallow from cattle and drippings from cooked lamb or mutton. But because tallow and rendered lamb/mutton grease aren't commercially available (or popular), in this book, I've focused on schmaltz rendered from roasted chicken along with lard/bacon drippings rendered from cooked bacon.

The next time you roast a chicken or cook some bacon, save your drippings! Both of these are primarily monounsaturated fats, while butter and ghee are saturated fats. All of these have a rich flavor that tends to make itself known, so it's best to use animal fats when you'd like them to lend their savoriness to your dish. (What doesn't taste fabulous cooked in butter or bacon drippings?)

Ghee is essentially clarified butter. It's butter that's been heated to allow the water content to evaporate (butter is about 18 percent water) and the milk solids to settle to the bottom and be discarded. What's left is butter oil. Because ghee is slightly higher in saturated fat than butter, it can handle higher heat. Ghee never spits or sputters, and it also has the most luscious buttery flavor imaginable. It greatly enhances any and every dish.

Oils at a Glance

SATURATED FATS

Oil	Heat	Type	Origin	Notes and Observations
Coconut oil	Medium-high	Tropical	Tropical countries, Southern Asia	This oil is faintly sweet, with a somewhat coconutty aroma that becomes more neutral when cooked.
Palm oil	Medium-high	Tropical	Brazil, tropical Africa, Southeast Asia, Malaysia, Indonesia	Also called dendê oil in Brazil, this deep red oil has an earthy flavor and will imbue any dish with a ruby-red color.
Palm kernel oil	High	Tropical	West Africa	This oil—pressed from the kernel of the palm fruit—is higher in saturated fat than palm oil; it's also nearly white in color.
Butter	Medium	Animal fat	Northern Europe (esp. Ireland and England), France, Poland, Italy, Scandinavia	Butter comes from many sources: goat, sheep, cow, buffalo (in Italy), even yak milk (as in Tibetan/Nepalese yak butter tea); grass-fed butter is lush-tasting and deep yellow.
Ghee	High	Animal fat	India, Nepal, Tibet, Bangladesh, Pakistan, North Africa	Essentially clarified butter, ghee handles very high heat and resists rancidity; smen, or fermented ghee, is popular in Northern Africa, while spiced fermented butter is made in Ethiopia and Somalia.

MONOUNSATURATED OILS

Oil	Heat	Type	Origin	Notes and Observations
Olive	Medium	Fruit	Mediterranean, Italy, Near East, California	Each extra-virgin olive oil has a distinct flavor, ranging from spicy to smooth and buttery.
Avocado	Medium	Fruit	Tropical countries, Mediterranean	The most neutral-tasting of all the oils, it's light-tasting and creamy.
Hazelnut	Medium	Nut	United States, France, Spain, Italy, Greece, Turkey	It's less overtly nutty-tasting than the other nut oils, but especially aromatic and smooth.
Peanut	Medium	Nut	China, West Africa, Southern United States, Southeast Asian	Very peanutty and incredibly aromatic when unheated, its flavor mellows considerably when heated.
Pecan	Medium	Nut	Mexico, United States	A delicate nut oil, this is one of the few that originates in North America.
Pistachio	Medium	Nut	Middle East (esp. Lebanon), Central Asia, Italy, California	With an assertive flavor, beautiful light-green color, and captivating aroma, you know it's pistachio right away.
Almond	Medium	Nut	Middle East, Southeast Asia, Iran, California	It's probably the mildest nut oil, with a light, almost-sweet scent.
Macadamia	Medium	Nut	Australia, Hawaii	There's no mistaking the macadamia flavor; this oil is great with tropical dishes.
Bacon drippings/lard	Medium	Animal Fat	Southern United States, France, Mexico, China, Central Europe, Scandinavia, Spain, Germany	Bacon drippings rendered from top-notch bacon tastes just as rich and savory as that top-notch bacon; lard varies in depth of flavor depending on how it was rendered, ranging from mostly neutral to almost bacon-flavored.
Schmaltz/ chicken fat/ goose fat/ duck fat	Medium	Animal Fat	Germany, Austria, Poland, Jewish traditional	Technically, schmaltz can also be drippings from a roasted goose or duck, but usually it's chicken, with a rich chicken essence that'll remind you of homemade broth.

POLYUNSATURATED OILS

Oil	Heat	Type	Origin	Notes and Observations
Walnut	None!	Nut	France, Australia, California	This oil has a strong yet delicate nutty aspect; roasted walnut oil tastes even more strongly of walnuts.
Flaxseed	None!	Seed	Central Europe	This oil is grassy and vegetal; herbal.
Hemp seed	None!	Seed	Canada, Australia, Europe	The flavor is a mix of grassy and nutty, with a beautiful green color. It's interchangeable with flaxseed oil.
Butternut squash seed	None!	Seed	New England	Fragrant and nutty, with more butteriness than pumpkin seed oil, it's a luscious drizzling oil.
Acorn squash seed	None!	Seed	New England	This oil is very similar to butternut squash seed oil, but it's a little sweeter and nuttier. It's interchangeable with butternut squash seed oil.
Kabocha squash seed	None!	Seed	New England	Reminiscent of the other squash seed oils, this oil has a hint of earthiness.
Sesame seed (toasted and untoasted)	Light	Seed	Middle East, Southeast Asia, China, Japan, Korea	Buttery and nutty, toasted sesame seed oil has a very pronounced flavor and is best used as a finishing drizzle.
Pumpkin seed	Light	Seed	Austria, Germany, Central Europe	This oil has a surprisingly strong nutty flavor and a beautiful deep orange color.

Oils Made Easy

Now let's talk about getting the good stuff: how and where to find unrefined oils. When you're scouring shelves for unrefined oils and fats, keep the following tips in mind:

- Look for oils that are packaged in opaque or dark-glass containers. They're protected from light.

- Avoid oils that have been stored beneath or next to direct sources of light and heat.

- Look for the word "unrefined." (See "Useful Terms" on page 28 for more information on labeling terms.)

- Opt for oils that clearly state their heat tolerance. For example, a good bottle of extra-virgin olive oil will probably tell you not to heat it over 325°F or 160°C.

- Avoid oils packaged in thin, clear plastic because such packaging indicates a low-quality oil.

- Try to buy oils at stores with high turnover. Many bottles are stamped with expiration dates, but even if they aren't, a bottle swathed in a thick layer of dust is not a good sign.

- If the oil is packaged in clear glass, check out the color. Unrefined oils each have their own hue, compared with refined oils, which are all the same shade of pale golden yellow.

Likely places to find unrefined oils include:

- Health-oriented stores

- Shops specializing in oils and vinegars

- In the "specialty" foods section of mainstream grocers, near where you'll often also find organic, gluten-free, whole-grain, etc. items.

- In a particularly well-stocked oils/baking aisle in a mainstream grocery store (although probably not in warehouse-style stores).

- Online "gourmet" foods retailers

- Websites of the manufacturers themselves

Some top-notch oil producers include:

- La Tourangelle: producers of unrefined hazelnut oil, almond oil, walnut oil, pistachio oil, sesame oil, avocado oil, peanut oil, pumpkinseed oil and coconut oil

- Spectrum Organics: sells a line of refined oils, but they also offer unrefined peanut oil, sesame oil, flaxseed oil, extra-virgin olive oil, etc. Just be sure to choose an oil that is clearly marked "unrefined" on the label

- Jungle Products: coconut and red palm oils

- Le Moulin de Marie: walnut and hazelnut oils

- Artisana Organic Foods: coconut oil

- Roland Foods: a nice variety of oils, plus some gluten-free grains and an exceptional assortment of global ingredients

- Tropical Traditions: offering a deliciously fragrant assortment of coconut products, from oil to flour to shredded coconut

- Stony Brook: specializing in squash seed oils such as kabocha, acorn and pumpkin

Time to Renovate the Pantry: Getting Rid of Common Refined Oils

TV chefs often exhort viewers to opt for oils such as canola and grape seed. "They're so neutral, you can use them with anything!" In this case, "neutral" means "has no flavor," and as you know by now, any oil without flavor is an oil that has been deodorized, which means that the flavor-free, aroma-free oil has been rendered rancid and was therefore in need of deodorizing. This is not a good choice for any dish.

Along with the negative health implications of eating rancid oils, loss of flavor is not a good thing from a culinary standpoint. Isn't the goal of cooking to create flavorful dishes? The dishes we're most drawn to are the ones that include the most prominent flavors. I bet you've never said to a waiter, "I'd like the most bland item on the menu, please." Let's embrace flavorful, unrefined oils. A slight drizzle of pistachio oil can transform a dish into something sublime. That's ditto for hazelnut, pumpkin seed or any other unrefined oil.

Of course, when using unrefined oils, it's crucial to know what their flavor profiles and individual heat-tolerance temperatures are. That's why you have this book! With this information at your fingertips, you can freely drizzle, pour and showcase your unrefined oils. And you can make sure you ditch the flavorless, unhealthy refined oils while you're at it.

The most common refined oils you'll see on the shelves are:

- **Canola:** This plant used to be known as rapeseed (it's still called that in some parts of the world), and the oil from its seeds was used as an industrial lubricant. Canadian scientists reengineered the rapeseed in the 1970s to make it edible for humans, hence its name "CAN(ada) O(il) L(ow) A(cid)." It's a widely grown cash crop, and the oil pressed from its seeds is typically a refined oil.

- **Corn:** Similar to soy, corn is a top GMO crop, and like soy, corn is a common "vegetable" oil. Theoretically, it's possible to find unrefined corn oil, but it's not likely.

- **Grape seed:** The seeds of grapes are so hard-hulled and contain so little oil—less than 10 percent—that heavy-duty machinery and industrial processing are needed to crush the seeds and extract the oil.

- **Rice bran:** This oil is pressed from the bran and germ of rice. Like corn oil, it's theoretically possible to find unrefined rice bran oil, but it's highly unlikely. And like corn oil, rice bran oil contains far more inflammatory omega-6 fats than anti-inflammatory omega-3 fats, which is not a healthy balance. (Although corn is far worse in terms of the omega-6 to omega-3 ratio.) It's used in Asian foods much the same way refined corn, soy and olive oils are used in Western foods—i.e., as a cheap "vegetable" oil.

- **Soy:** Soy is a top genetically modified organism (GMO) crop, and soy contains goitrogenic compounds that impair thyroid function. (That's especially bad news for women, who typically experience more cases of hypothyroidism than men do.) Soy is often sold under the catchall term of "vegetable oil." Calling an oil "vegetable oil" allows manufacturers to use whatever oil is cheapest at the time without having to go to the expense of changing the labeling.

- **Safflower:** This oil tends to pop up in chips and snack foods. It is refined, and safflower oil also contains zero omega-3 oils but plenty of omega-6s, which means it's a highly inflammatory oil. (See the sections on omega-3 and omega-6 fats on pages 20–22 for more information.)

- **Sunflower:** This oil is less common and is theoretically more likely to be unrefined than the other oils in this list, but the vast majority of sunflower oil is tasteless, odorless and the same bland golden hue as all of the other refined oils.

The following oils are commonly found in unrefined and refined versions. So make sure you look for the unrefined versions:

- **Almond:** It's just as common to find refined as unrefined versions of this oil, so double-check labels. You'll know you have the good stuff the instant you unscrew the top of the bottle and breathe in the fragrant, unmistakable scent of almonds.

- **Coconut:** While most coconut oils are labeled "virgin" or "unrefined" and truly are, some are refined into flavorless, odorless oblivion. Buyer, beware!

- **Palm and palm kernel:** Because palm oil (remember, that's derived from the palm fruit itself, while palm kernel oil is pressed from the kernel of the fruit) has such a bright-red color and distinct earthy taste, products marked "palm oil" are almost always made of palm oil that has been heavily refined to get rid of its unique characteristics. Palm kernel oil is less likely to have been refined because it's an unsaturated fat and therefore far more stable to begin with. However, both kinds of palm oil are generally incorporated into multi-oil products that contain refined oils, such as canola and various "vegetable" oils. Always look for palm oil clearly labeled as "unrefined" or "virgin."

- **Peanut:** You'll know the unrefined version by its rich mahogany color and its powerful peanutty flavor and aroma. Look for the word "unrefined" on the label.

- **Olive:** Always, always seek out extra-virgin olive oils from reputable oil manufacturers, such as California Olive Ranch. Real olive oil will vary in flavor, color and aroma—just as the actual olives do!

- **Sesame:** It's relatively easy to find sesame and toasted sesame oils marked "unrefined," but always double-check. Some sesame oils are refined because they're intended for high-heat wok cooking. Unrefined sesame oil can't handle much heat at all. It's never a good idea to use refined oil, so if you want to do high-heat wok cooking, coconut would be a lovely oil to use.

- **Walnut:** Because unrefined walnut oil is so delicate—it's an omega-3–rich polyunsaturated oil—it's often refined to "lengthen" its shelf life. Unrefined walnut is incredibly nutty and rich-tasting.

Substituting Oils and Fats

While the intent of this book is to introduce you to a wide variety of unrefined oils and fats, you might not be able to find all of the oils mentioned in this book. Fear not! You can easily swap out one oil or fat for another. Remember, the most important aspect of any given oil or fat is its heat tolerance. (The second-most important aspect is flavor.) So once you know how much you want to heat an oil, you can choose from a variety of suitable oils.

For example, if you don't have almond or avocado oil, use extra-virgin olive oil instead. It's a monounsaturated fat, too. If you don't have palm oil, use another saturated fat such as butter or coconut oil. Out of walnut oil? Use flaxseed oil, which is another polyunsaturated fat. Check out this cheat sheet to see what's interchangeable.

Quick List of Substitutions

High heat: Use butter, coconut oil or palm oil. Palm kernel oil and ghee handle the highest heat of all. (Note that butter will brown quickly at high heat. That's because unlike ghee, butter contains milk solids, and those are affected by heat.)

Medium heat: Use extra-virgin olive oil, avocado oil, peanut oil, hazelnut oil, almond oil, pistachio oil, macadamia oil, pecan oil, bacon drippings or rendered fat from chicken, goose or duck. (Chicken fat is often called "schmaltz.")

Low heat: Use sesame oil, toasted sesame oil or pumpkin seed oil.

No heat: Use walnut oil, flaxseed oil, hemp seed oil, butternut squash seed oil, acorn squash seed oil or kabocha squash seed oil.

The Recipes

It's time to taste the full flavors of unrefined oils. Whether you have grass-fed butter and a bottle of extra-virgin olive oil on hand or your collection of oils occupies an entire shelf, you're about to find plenty of inspiring recipes to try.

To make it even easier to explore the world of unrefined oils, the recipes are organized by type of oil they use: saturated, monounsaturated and polyunsaturated. That makes it easy to swap one oil for another. Experiment with different oils in the same recipe to see which you like best. You'll love the rich accents unrefined oils lend to any dish. Now, let's get cooking!

Recipes with Saturated Fats: Go Ahead and Turn Up the Heat!

Coconut Oil, Ghee and Red Palm Oil

Not too many fats fall into the saturated category, but the few that do are valuable ingredients for cooking and baking. That's because saturated fats are the sturdiest fats of all, which means you can use them to cook at high heat, plus they're good for roasting, which is typically done at 400°F (200°C).

Because saturated fats are so sturdy and shelf-stable, they don't need to be refrigerated. Butter, though, will last markedly longer when refrigerated, particularly if you live in a hot climate. Coconut oil, ghee and palm oil can be kept in a cool, dark cupboard.

Of the saturated fats, ghee can handle the highest heat. Ghee is also known as "clarified" or "drawn" butter. When butter is simmered so that the milk solids fall to the bottom and the water content evaporates, you get ghee. Why does it react so differently to heat? Because the water portion of butter is what starts to steam and pop around 212°F (100°C), and the milk solids burn when overheated, when you remove those two components, the remaining ghee can handle 500°F (260°C). Not even coconut or palm oil can go up to those temperatures, although palm kernel oil comes close. Of course, when you upgrade your animal products to grass-fed varieties, you don't need to crank up the burner to high because grass-fed products cook at half the heat and half the time of their conventional counterparts. But if you do find yourself in a situation requiring high heat, now you know what to use!

Recipe Tips: A "dollop" or "spoonful" of coconut or palm oil called for in a recipe means about 1 tablespoon (12 g). A "knob" of ghee is a tablespoon. All herbs are dried unless listed as fresh.

Zucchini Blossoms Stuffed with Capers and Goat Cheese

Makes about 12 blossoms

Zucchini blossoms are delicate and don't last long, but they make elegant vessels for this goat-cheese-and-caper blend. If you grow your own zucchini, you'll have plenty of blossoms to stuff with delicious fillings, or you may be able to find just-picked blossoms at a farmers' market. Each blossom is a potential squash, so harvesting blossoms does mean sacrificing eventual zucchini. But zucchini plants are so prolific that you can snip a few blossoms and still wind up with a bumper crop of zucchini. The mild vegetal flavor of the blossoms allows them to complement any filling.

About 12 fresh zucchini blossoms
Coconut oil for cooking
1 red bell pepper, stem and seeds removed, flesh minced
1 small onion, minced
2 cloves garlic, minced
4 ounces (110 g) goat cheese
1 tablespoon (8.6 g) capers, drained

Choose blossoms that have fully opened but have not yet begun to wilt. (When they wilt, they become so limp that they're impossible to work with.) Snip off the blossoms right at the base, and then rinse them with cold water and carefully reach into the centers to check for critters and to pull out the pistils. Set aside the cleaned blossoms while you make the stuffing.

In a medium skillet, melt a generous dollop of oil over medium heat. Stir in the pepper and onion and cook for 3 minutes, or until the onion turns translucent, stirring often. Stir in the garlic and continue to cook for an additional 2 minutes, or until the garlic is fragrant. Remove from the heat and stir in the goat cheese and capers.

Working with one blossom at a time, use a small spoon or your fingers to split apart the petals and slide about 1 tablespoon (15 g) of stuffing into each blossom. "Seal" each one by gently twisting the petals together at the top of the blossom to form a closed package.

In a fresh skillet, melt another dollop of oil over medium heat. Add the stuffed blossoms, cooking them in batches so as not to overcrowd the skillet. Cook them just long enough for the blossoms to become golden brown on both sides. (It only takes a minute or two!) Shake the skillet often to move the blossoms around and prevent them from burning. These tender blossoms are best served immediately.

Bacon-Chocolate Pancakes

Makes 12 pancakes

Bacon-studded chocolate bars have become de rigueur, but what about pancakes studded with bacon and chocolate? Talk about a good reason to get up! Even if you don't have already-cooked bacon in your fridge, it only takes 20 minutes of non-messy oven time to have perfectly crisp bacon to crumble into the batter. Then you just have to do a little whisking and flipping to have twelve little cakes of edible heaven. If you have any leftover pancakes, the next day, warm them in a toaster oven for a quick breakfast. These pancakes are so much better than sugary cereal! Besides, the coconut oil adds a hint of natural sweetness.

½ cup (62 g) quinoa flour*
½ cup (45 g) almond flour
½ cup (30 g) buckwheat, teff or brown rice flour*
2 to 4 ounces (58 to 115 g) 85 percent dark chocolate, chopped, depending on how chocolaty you want your pancakes to be (You can use 75 percent if you prefer less-dark chocolate.)
1 teaspoon baking powder
½ teaspoon baking soda
Pinch sea salt
4 eggs
4 strips cooked bacon, chopped
½ cup + 2 tablespoons (150 ml) buttermilk**
1 tablespoon (15 ml) maple syrup + more for serving
Coconut oil for cooking

In a large bowl, whisk together the flours, chocolate, baking powder, baking soda and salt.

In a smaller bowl, whisk together the eggs, bacon, buttermilk and maple syrup. Whisk the egg mixture into the dry ingredients, mixing well.

In a large skillet or griddle pan, heat a spoonful of oil over medium heat. Add batter to the skillet in ¼ cupfuls (60 ml), making 3 or 4 pancakes per batch (or whatever comfortably fits your skillet). Cook for 3 minutes, or until you see bubbles on the tops and the bottoms are golden brown. Gently flip each pancake and cook for another 2 minutes, or until both sides are golden brown.

Transfer the pancakes to a wire rack. Wipe the pan with a paper towel after each batch. You'll probably have chocolate in the pan, and you don't want that to scorch. Add more oil and repeat until all of the pancakes are cooked. Serve them with a drizzle of maple syrup if you like.

Leftover pancakes can be refrigerated for 5 days.

These flours aren't Paleo, but they are gluten-free and whole-grain.

**To make this dish more Paleo-friendly, use ½ cup (120 ml) whole coconut milk and 1 teaspoon lemon juice in place of the buttermilk.*

Coconut-Roasted Spicy Beernuts

Makes 2 cups (280 g) nuts

Beernuts are usually made with peanuts, but you can make any nut into a beernut by roasting it with coconut oil and spices. Almonds and cashews work nicely. They are about the same size as peanuts, and they're mild-tasting, so they pair well with just about any spice. You can either blend your own berbere mixture (adding as much cayenne as you like) or you can use chili powder for these spicy beernuts. Be sure to flip the nuts over to prevent the spices from scorching. Using parchment paper rather than aluminum foil will help prevent the nuts from sticking to the pan, and it will make them easier to flip.

2 tablespoons (30 ml) melted coconut oil

2 cups (280 g) raw whole cashews or almonds (or a mixture of both)

1 tablespoon (7 g) berbere or chili powder (see page 117)

Dash sea salt (unless the spice blend is already salty)

Preheat the oven to 300°F (150°C) and line a rimmed baking sheet with parchment paper.

Make sure the oil is free-flowing. (Gently warm it if necessary.) In a medium bowl, mix all of the ingredients. Spread the mixture on the prepared baking sheet and roast for 20 minutes, flipping the nuts over halfway through the cooking time, or until the nuts are turning an even golden brown.

Cover a clean plate with a paper towel and transfer the roasted nuts to the plate to allow them to cool.

Butternut-Cashew Spiced Muffins

Makes 12 muffins

Thanks to their mildly sweet flavor, cashews make a great flour. They're also less oily than many other nuts—walnuts and pecans are prone to becoming nut butter, not flour—so it's a snap to grind raw or dry-roasted cashews into flour. High-speed blenders and flour mills are the best way to transform cashews into silky-smooth, fine-grained flour. Or, if you have a mini food processor or coffee grinder, you can chop the cashews first, and then grind them into cashew meal. ("Meal" means coarsely ground flour.) Either way, the sweetness of the cashews and the sweet potato flour will be a delicious contrast to the tart cranberries.

1¼ cups (150 g) raw or roasted cashew flour

½ cup (56 g) sweet potato flour

2 teaspoons (9.2 g) baking powder

1 teaspoon cinnamon

½ teaspoon ginger

½ teaspoon sea salt

½ cup (123 g) cooked and mashed butternut squash (canned or freshly cooked and pureed)

½ cup (120 ml) melted coconut oil

¼ cup (60 ml) maple syrup

2 eggs

1 cup (100 g) cranberries (thawed if frozen)

Preheat the oven to 400°F (200°C) and line a 12-cup muffin tin with parchment paper cups.

In a large bowl, whisk together the flours, baking powder, cinnamon, ginger and salt.

In a medium bowl, whisk together the butternut squash, oil, maple syrup and eggs. Whisk the wet ingredients into the dry ingredients, and then stir in the cranberries.

Fill each muffin cup ⅔ full with batter. Bake for 20 minutes, or until an inserted toothpick comes out clean.

Butternut- and Beef-Stuffed Spanish Peppers

Makes 4 servings

Fun veggie fact: Red, orange, yellow and green bell peppers are all the same plant, just at different stages of ripeness. Green peppers are the least ripe and therefore the least sweet; red peppers are the ripest and sweetest. Orange and yellow fall in between. You could make this recipe rainbow-style and stuff a pepper of each color. It's a culinary mix-and-match! Sweet paprika is made of dried and ground red bell peppers, so you'll have a double-pepper effect no matter which color(s) you choose.

1 small butternut squash, skin trimmed away and seeds discarded, flesh cut into ½" (1.2 cm) cubes
4 large bell peppers of whatever color you like best
Coconut oil for cooking
1 medium yellow onion, chopped
1 small zucchini or yellow squash, diced
4 cloves garlic, chopped
1 pound (448 g) ground beef
2 tablespoons (15 g) sweet paprika
1 tablespoon (3 g) thyme
1 teaspoon rosemary
Dash sea salt
1 egg, lightly whisked with a fork
Grated Monterey Jack cheese for topping*

Preheat the oven to 375°F (190°C) and cover a rimmed baking sheet with parchment paper.

Fill a large pot halfway with water and bring to a boil. Add the squash and simmer for 5 minutes. Drain well. Slice the peppers in half—leave the stems on for a prettier look—and clean out the seeds and ribs.

In a large skillet, melt a dollop of oil over medium heat. Add the onion and zucchini and cook for 5 minutes, or until the onion is starting to turn translucent. Add the garlic, beef, paprika, thyme, rosemary and salt and continue cooking for another 4 to 5 minutes, stirring often to break up the beef, or until the beef is opaque and cooked through.

Scoop the beef and veggies into a large bowl and add the squash and egg. Mix well. Spoon the filling into the peppers and place the peppers on the prepared baking sheet. Top the peppers with the cheese and bake them for 25 minutes, or until the cheese is golden brown and bubbly.

For a Paleo-friendly dish, omit the cheese.

Pecan-Crusted Salmon with Herb and Garlic Rutabaga Oven Fries

Makes 4 servings

For this salmon recipe, you'll be taking advantage of the cooking power of coconut oil and the nutty flavor of unheated pecan oil. Most nut oils can handle a little heat, but because you'll be cooking the salmon for about 15 minutes, it's best to use heat-stable coconut oil to sear the salmon, and then savor the richness of the pecan oil post-cooking. There's no need to worry about competing flavors. The delicate, smooth flavor of coconut oil provides a gentle undertone to the full flavors of the rich pecans and fresh-from-the-sea wild salmon.

FOR THE FRIES

1 large rutabaga (about 3 pounds [1,350 g])

4 cloves garlic, chopped

1 bunch cilantro, leaves only, chopped

½ teaspoon sea salt

2 tablespoons (30 ml) warmed coconut oil

FOR THE SALMON

¾ cup (75 g) pecan halves, roughly chopped

¼ teaspoon sea salt

1½ pounds (672 g) wild salmon filets, rinsed and patted dry

Coconut oil for cooking

Pecan oil for finishing

FOR THE DIPPING SAUCE*

¾ cup (173 ml) plain whole-milk Greek yogurt

¼ cup (60 ml) Dijon mustard

*For a Paleo-friendly dish, omit the dipping sauce.

To make the fries, arrange the oven racks so that they're positioned in the upper and lower thirds of the oven. Preheat the oven to 425°F (220°C) and line 2 baking sheets with parchment paper.

Cut the rutabaga in half, and then trim away the tough outer skin. Cut the halves into ½" (1.2 cm-) thick sticks. Place them in a large bowl and toss well with the garlic, cilantro, salt and oil. Spread them out on the prepared baking sheets, trying not to overlap any of the fries. Bake for 15 minutes, and then rotate the baking sheets, placing the topmost sheet on the lowermost rack and vice versa. Continue to bake for 15 additional minutes. Flip the fries over, and then return them to the oven for a final 10 minutes of baking. (They should be well browned.)

While the fries bake, prepare the salmon. Place the pecans and salt in a coffee grinder or small food processor and grind them for a few seconds in bursts, just long enough to create crumbs. (If you process them any longer, you'll have pecan butter.) Place the salmon on a non-porous cutting board—don't use a wooden one because they're harder to clean—with the skin side down. If necessary, cut the filets into smaller pieces that fit into your skillet. Gently press the pecan crumbs into the non-skin side of the filets.

In a large skillet, melt the coconut oil over medium heat. Gently place the salmon filets skin-side-up in the skillet. Cook for 3 minutes. Carefully flip the filets over—try not to dislodge the pecan crumbs—and cover the skillet. Reduce the heat to medium-low. Cook for 10 minutes, or until the salmon flakes easily at the thickest part and is opaque all the way through.

While the salmon cooks, make the dip. In a small mixing bowl, stir together the yogurt and mustard.

Before serving the salmon, drizzle them with the pecan oil. Serve with the rutabaga fries and a small bowl of the dip.

New Orleans Muffaletta Scramble

Makes 4 servings

Traditionally, "muffaletta" describes a type of sandwich, but the same ingredients that go into the signature New Orleans sandwich make a great scramble. It's all about the cured meats, cheese and pickled veggies! Giardiniera literally means "mixed vegetables," and that's what it is: a blend of cauliflower, peppers, pearl onions and cucumbers that have been packed with vinegar and herbs. Embellishing the giardiniera with some olives and capers makes these scrambles even more savory. This muffaletta is so easy to make that every day feels like Mardi Gras!

YOUR CHOICE OF CHEESE*

2 to 4 ounces (56 to 112 g) provolone cheese, sliced into ribbons
2 to 4 ounces (56 to 112 g) mozzarella cheese, sliced into ribbons

YOUR CHOICE OF PICKLED VEGGIES

Handful sliced pitted olives, either green or black
Several seeded pepperoncini, chopped
1 to 2 tablespoons (8.6 to 17.2 g) capers, drained
1 cup (140 g) chopped and drained giardiniera (mix of pickled Italian veggies)
1 cup (300 g) brined artichokes, chopped and drained

YOUR CHOICE OF MEAT

2 to 4 ounces (56 to 112 g) sliced ham, cut into ribbons
2 to 4 ounces (56 to 112 g) sliced salami, cut into ribbons
2 to 4 ounces (56 to 112 g) sliced mortadella, cut into ribbons

6 eggs + more if desired
½ cup (120 ml) whole milk*
Coconut oil for cooking

In a large bowl, place your choices of cheese, veggies and meat. Add the eggs, pour in the milk and then whisk to combine well. If you've added so many optional ingredients that you can barely see any eggs, whisk in another egg or two to balance out the cheeses/veggies/meats.

In a 10" (25 cm) skillet, heat a generous dollop of oil over medium heat. Pour in the egg mixture and let cook undisturbed for 5 minutes. With a spatula, gently drag the edges down and into the center, and then let cook another few minutes before moving the eggs around again gently, lifting them to allow any uncooked portions to run beneath the spatula and onto the hot surface of the skillet. When the eggs are opaque but fluffy, remove the skillet from the heat. (The eggs will look a little bit like puffy clouds.) Serve the scramble immediately.

Leftover scramble can be refrigerated for 4 days.

*To make this dish Paleo-friendly, omit the cheese and use coconut milk in place of dairy milk.

Brazil Nut Pesto Chicken with Toasted Wild Rice and Coconut

Makes 4 servings

When we think of nuts, we usually think of peanuts or almonds or cashews, or maybe walnuts or pecans. Brazil nuts are probably the least-thought-of nut. That's a shame because Brazil nuts are chock-full of selenium, and they also have a very rich, buttery flavor. (Although it's worth pointing out that Brazil nuts are also a common allergen, so always check with your guests before serving a dish with Brazil nuts.) Thanks to their lushness, Brazil nuts provide a creamy flavor that works beautifully in raw desserts and non-dairy ice cream. For an extra-decadent dessert, try dipping Brazil nuts in melted dark chocolate. Or use them in a savory recipe like this one.

¾ cup (120 g) wild rice
½ cup (43 g) unsweetened coconut flakes
2 cups (480 ml) chicken broth
½ cup (120 ml) water
Coconut oil for cooking
10 cloves garlic, chopped
¾ cup (84 g) Brazil nuts, chopped
½ cup (12 g) lightly packed fresh basil leaves
Dash sea salt
1½ pounds (672 g) boneless skinless chicken breast, trimmed, cut into 1" (2.5 cm-) thick strips

In a large skillet, place the rice over medium heat. Toast for 10 minutes, or until the wild rice is turning golden brown and is fragrant. Remove the rice to a cool plate. Add the coconut flakes to the same skillet and return to medium heat. Toast for 2 to 3 minutes, shaking the skillet once or twice, or until the coconut is turning golden brown. Transfer the coconut to another cool plate.

In a medium pot, bring the broth and water to a boil. Reduce the heat to low, add the rice and simmer for 40 minutes, or until the grains have begun to swell and split and they've reached their desired tenderness. Drain well.

To make the pesto, in a large skillet, melt about 1 tablespoon (12 g) oil over medium-low heat. Add the garlic and cook, stirring often, for 3 to 4 minutes, or until the garlic is beginning to turn golden brown. Transfer the garlic to a food processor. Add the nuts, basil and salt and process until well blended. (If the pesto looks dry, blend in a little more melted oil.)

In the same skillet, heat another tablespoonful (12 g) of oil over medium heat. Add the chicken and cook, flipping the chicken occasionally, for 7 to 8 minutes, or until the thickest piece is opaque all the way through when cut in half. Remove the chicken from the heat and toss with the pesto, toasted coconut and cooked rice.
Serve immediately.

Leftover chicken can be refrigerated for 4 days. The basil will darken, but that won't affect its flavor.

Szechuan Beef, Scallion and Bamboo Stir-Fry with Kelp Noodles

Makes 4 servings

If you've never come across kelp noodles before, you're in for a treat. They look a bit like glass noodles, but instead of being made with bean starch, kelp noodles are made with—you guessed it—kelp. Seaweed is notoriously good at making things stick together, so it shouldn't come as a surprise that someone thought to make seaweed into noodles. Kelp noodles have a firm texture and faintly briny taste that pairs beautifully with savory broccoli and beef. Look for kelp noodles in the refrigerated section of health-oriented stores. Sliced bamboo adds another layer of exotic flavor, but if you can't find bamboo, opt for water chestnuts, which is another classic Asian ingredient.

1 head broccoli, florets only
Coconut oil for cooking
1 red bell pepper, seeds and stem removed, flesh cut into thin strips
6 green onions, trimmed and minced
8 cloves garlic, chopped
1½ cups (360 ml) chicken broth
8 ounces (224 g) sliced bamboo, drained
2 tablespoons (40 ml) honey
2 tablespoons (30 ml) gluten-free tamari*
Sprinkling of crushed red pepper flakes
2 tablespoons (14 g) coconut flour
1 pound (448 g) top sirloin, trimmed and cut into ½" (1.2 cm-) thick strips
12 ounces (340 g) kelp noodles, rinsed in cool water and drained well
Bean sprouts for garnishing

Fill a large pot halfway with water and bring to a boil. Add the broccoli and simmer for 5 minutes. Drain well.

In a large skillet, heat a generous spoonful of oil over medium heat. Add the bell pepper and cook, stirring occasionally, for 5 minutes. Reduce the heat to medium-low, stir in the green onion and garlic, and continue cooking for an additional 5 minutes.

Stir in the broth, bamboo, honey, tamari, red pepper flakes and flour. Increase the heat to medium. Stir in the sirloin and cook for 5 minutes, or until the sirloin has reached the desired doneness, flipping the sirloin over halfway through to make sure it cooks evenly. Remove the skillet from the heat and stir in the drained noodles. Serve immediately, garnishing each portion with the sprouts.

Leftover stir-fry can be refrigerated for 4 days.

For a Paleo-friendly dish, use liquid amino acids in place of the tamari.

Island Alfredo Mahi-Mahi with Amp-It-Up Mango and Black-Eyed Pea Salad

Makes 4 servings

Depending on how much you want to amp up your salad, you can vary the amount and type of pepper you use. If you were in the islands, you might get a Scotch bonnet pepper with your mahi-mahi. Now, that's hot! Red pepper flakes aren't very high on the Scoville heat scale, so you might instead want to use fresh bird's-eye peppers, jalapeños or whatever tickles your heat-loving taste buds. Or you can smash fresh jalapeños peppers to crush their inner ribs and release more capsicum, which is the compound responsible for the burn. Now you know how to amp up anything you make! If you're a fan of milder fare, go easy on the red pepper flakes and let the coconut oil and cream counter the heat with their beat-the-heat richness.

FOR THE SALAD

Coconut oil for cooking
1 red bell pepper, stem and seeds removed, flesh chopped
4 green onions, trimmed and minced
4 cloves garlic, chopped
Dash crushed red pepper flakes
1 tablespoon (3 g) thyme
1 teaspoon nutmeg
1 teaspoon sea salt
1 mango, flesh only, chopped
15 ounces (425 g) black-eyed peas, drained*

FOR THE MAHI-MAHI

Coconut oil for cooking
1½ to 2 pounds (672 to 896 g) mahi-mahi, rinsed and patted dry
At least ½ cup (120 g) Coconut Cream (see page 111)
Sea salt for sprinkling

To make the salad, in a medium skillet, heat a generous dollop of oil over medium heat. Add the bell pepper and onions and cook, stirring often, for 5 minutes. Stir in the garlic, red pepper flakes, thyme, nutmeg and salt and continue to cook for an additional 3 minutes, stirring often, or until the garlic is softened and fragrant. Transfer the mixture to a large bowl and stir in the mango and peas. Set aside while you make the mahi-mahi.

To make the mahi-mahi, in a large skillet, heat a generous dollop of oil over medium heat. Add the mahi-mahi with the skin side up. Cover the skillet and cook for 5 minutes. Move the skillet off of the heat, and then carefully flip over the mahi-mahi. Re-cover and continue to cook on medium heat for an additional 3 minutes. Reduce the heat to medium-low and cook for a final 3 minutes, or until the thickest part of the mahi-mahi flakes cleanly and is opaque. Use two forks to pull apart the fish to see if it flakes.

Top each portion of mahi-mahi with a spoonful of Coconut Cream and a sprinkling of salt. Serve with a side of the salad.

Leftover mahi-mahi can be refrigerated for 1 day, while the leftover salad can be refrigerated for 4 days.

If you want a Paleo-friendly dish, substitute green peas for the black-eyed peas.

Slow-Cooked Lamb with Braised Fennel and Smashed Rutabaga

Makes 4 servings plus plenty of extra shredded lamb

When you're preparing a large cut of meat such as a shoulder or leg, a slow cooker is the way to go. There's no need to baste, braise or even do any trimming. The fat will rise to the top, and you can skim it off and discard it later if you like. The slow-cooker method is easy and foolproof, and also the meat will be so tender that it will nearly fall off of the bone. You can serve it as intact portions or shred it and include the shredded meat in everything from stews to casseroles to wraps. Looking for a better-quality alternative to lunchmeat? You've just made it.

3 pounds (1.3 kg) boneless lamb shoulder
8 cloves garlic, chopped
1 tablespoon (3 g) rosemary
1 teaspoon sea salt, plus more for sprinkling
4 cups (60 ml) chicken broth
1 fennel bulb, fronds trimmed away and any tough outer stalks removed
Coconut oil for roasting
1 rutabaga, peeled and cut into 1" (2.5 cm) cubes
Ghee for seasoning

In a 6-quart (5.7 L) slow cooker, place the lamb, garlic, rosemary and 1 teaspoon of salt. Pour in the broth and cook on high for 5 hours. (The meat should start to shred into pieces when you lift it up.)

Turn off the cooker. Using tongs, remove the meat to a plate. Let the lamb cool until you can comfortably touch it. Use your fingertips (or two forks) to shred the meat into bite-sized pieces. (If you're not going to use it all right away, you might want to leave the leftover meat as hunks rather than shredded. That way, the leftover lamb will be moister.)

During the final hour of slow-cooking the lamb, make the veggies. Preheat the oven to 375°F (190°C) and cover a baking sheet with parchment paper. Cut off the bottom of the fennel bulb and discard it, and then cut the fennel into long slices lengthwise, cutting from the base of each stalk to the bottom of the bulb. Arrange the fennel pieces on the prepared baking sheet so that they don't overlap. Spoon a dab of coconut oil onto each piece of fennel and rub the oil onto each one to coat it. Bake for 30 minutes, or until fennel is fragrant and turning light brown.

To make the rutabaga, fill a large pot halfway with water and bring to a boil. Add the rutabaga and reduce the heat to medium. Simmer for 25 minutes, or until you can easily pierce the rutabaga cubes with the tip of a sharp knife. Drain well.

Put the rutabaga back into the still-warm empty pot and add a generous knob of ghee and a sprinkling of salt. Using a potato masher, mash well to combine. (Or, if you want fluffy rutabaga, run it through a food processor.) Serve the lamb with the fennel and smashed rutabaga.

Leftovers can be refrigerated for 4 days.

Mini Crab Cakes with Fried Nori Strips and Chow Mein Noodles

Makes 4 servings (about 2 ½ cakes apiece)

When you were a kid, did you love those crunchy noodles that came in a can, the cute little strands that seemed to be the Asian equivalent of croutons? Well, you can make your own: Just fry some freshly cooked noodles in coconut oil until they're crisp. Eat them promptly. If you wait too long, the noodles will soften and you'll lose that classic chow mein texture. You can find sheets of nori in Japanese grocery stores or in well-stocked mainstream markets in the Asian foods section.

Coconut oil for cooking
½ large red bell pepper, seeds and stem removed, flesh minced
3 cloves garlic, minced
1 bunch chives, snipped or minced (about ¼ cup [12 g])
2 tablespoons (26 ml) stone-ground mustard
2 teaspoons (2 g) dill
½ teaspoon sea salt
1 egg
12 ounces (336 g) crabmeat, pressed firmly and drained well
1¼ to 1½ cups (113 to 135 g) almond flour
4 ounces (114 g) brown rice spaghetti*
4 sheets nori, cut into 1½" (4 cm-) thick strips

*Brown rice is not a Paleo ingredient, but it is whole-grain and gluten-free.

In a medium skillet, heat a spoonful of oil over medium heat. Add the peppers and cook, stirring occasionally, for 3 minutes, or until softened. Stir in the garlic and continue to cook for another 2 minutes, or until the garlic is soft and fragrant. Transfer the mixture to a large bowl and add the chives, mustard, dill, salt, egg and crabmeat. Add 1¼ cups (113 g) almond flour and mix well to combine. (If the mixture is too wet to shape into cakes, add the remaining ¼ cup [22 g] flour or more, if needed and mix again.)

To make the cakes, use a ¼ cup (60 ml) measure to scoop out the crab mixture. Firmly press it into the measuring cup, and then tap it out into your hand. Gently press the cake into a patty and set it on a large plate or cutting board. Repeat with the remaining crab to make 10 cakes.

Coat the bottom of a large skillet with a generous tablespoon (15 ml) of oil and place over medium heat. Add the crab cakes—don't overcrowd the pan—and gently flatten them slightly with a spatula. Cook for 3 to 4 minutes, and then gently flip over the cakes. Continue cooking another 3 to 4 minutes, or until the cakes are golden brown on both sides. Remove the cakes to a plate and continue to cook the remaining cakes, wiping the skillet clean and adding fresh oil between batches. After you have cooked all of the cakes, wipe the skillet clean again so you can use it later.

While the cakes are cooking, prepare the pasta according to the package directions, and then drain it well. Place the pasta in the same skillet you used for the crab cakes, add a generous spoonful of oil and a sprinkling of salt, and cook over medium heat for 10 minutes, occasionally moving the pasta around with the tongs. (The pasta should be crisp and turning golden brown.)

While the pasta cooks, heat a generous spoonful of oil in the medium skillet you used for cooking the pepper and garlic. Add the nori strips, pressing each into the oil with the tongs to coat it. Cook over medium-low heat for 5 minutes or until the nori is turning golden brown. Work in batches if necessary, adding more oil to the skillet when needed. Transfer the cooked nori to a plate. Immediately serve the crispy fried noodles topped with the crab cakes. Place the nori on top. If you like, you can crumble the nori strips first.

Baked Whitefish with Pineapple and Lemon Salsa and Crispy Quinoa

Makes 4 servings

Many people find the idea of making fish intimidating. It isn't! On the contrary, fish is easier to cook than meat because fish filets are more uniformly thick (which means they cook more evenly) and it's so easy to check the doneness of fish (just flake apart the center with a fork to see if it's opaque). Baking fish in the oven takes even less effort than cooking it on the stove. While the whitefish in this recipe happily bakes, the quinoa can simmer and you can chop the ingredients for the salsa. If you're in a huge hurry, you can skip sautéing the quinoa, but the crunchy texture of sautéed quinoa contrasts nicely with the tender baked fish and juicy salsa.

FOR THE QUINOA

2 cups (470 ml) water
¾ cup (130 g) quinoa
Coconut oil for crisping

FOR THE FISH

Coconut oil for baking
1½ pounds (672 g) whitefish (such as grouper, snapper, roughy or cod), with or without skin, rinsed in cold water and patted dry
Sea salt for sprinkling

FOR THE SALSA

½ small pineapple, peeled and cut into small cubes
12 to 16 cherry tomatoes, cut in half or quartered
2 green onions, green part only, minced
1 small bunch cilantro, leaves only, chopped
Juice of ½ lemon

Preheat the oven to 350°F (180°C).

In a medium pot, bring the water to a boil. Add the quinoa and reduce the heat to medium-low. Simmer uncovered for 15 minutes, and then drain the quinoa well. Transfer the quinoa to a large skillet and add enough oil to coat the quinoa. Cook over medium heat, stirring often, for 10 minutes, or until the quinoa is becoming crisp. Remove the skillet from the heat.

While the quinoa simmers, make the fish: Drizzle a spoonful of oil into a glass baking dish. (You'll probably need a 9" x 13" [23 cm x 33 cm] dish to accommodate the fish, or you may be able to cut the filets in half and arrange them to fit into a smaller dish.)

Rub each piece of fish with oil and position them skin-side-down (if they have skin) in a single layer. Sprinkle the fish with salt and spoon a little more oil on top if the filets look dry. Bake for 20 minutes, or until the thickest filet is opaque when flaked apart with a fork.

While the fish bakes, make the salsa: In a medium bowl, place the pineapple, tomatoes, green onions, cilantro and lemon juice and stir well to combine. Serve the fish accompanied with a side of crispy quinoa and the salsa.

Leftover fish can be refrigerated for 1 day, while the quinoa and salsa can be refrigerated for 3 days.

Costa Rican Picadillo with Tostones

Makes 4 servings

You know you're in for a treat when a Costa Rican family serves picadillo with a side of piping-hot tostones. While gallo pinto may be the national dish, picadillo is made for special occasions. To do the dish justice, the cook takes the time to mince all of the veggies so that the final dish is a gorgeous rainbow of confetti. Some cooks may also finely chop the beef, but in this recipe, you'll be using ground beef as an easy timesaver. The slightly sweet flavor of the coconut oil complements the savory beef and underscores the slight sweetness of the veggies and semi-ripe plantains. If you happen to have any leftover tostones—unlikely!—you can reheat them by quickly sautéing them in a fresh dollop of coconut oil to restore their crispness.

FOR THE PICADILLO

1 pound (448 g) sweet potatoes, trimmed but not peeled, cut into ¼" (6 mm) cubes
Coconut oil for cooking
1 onion, chopped
1 red bell pepper, seeds and stem discarded, flesh minced
1 zucchini, minced
3 ribs celery, minced
1 large tomato, chopped
2 tablespoons (14 g) cumin
1 teaspoon sea salt
1 pound (448 g) ground beef
1 small bunch cilantro, leaves only, chopped

FOR THE TOSTONES

2 greenish-yellow plantains
Coconut oil for cooking
Sea salt for sprinkling

To make the picadillo, fill a large pot halfway with water and bring it to a boil. Add the potatoes and reduce the heat to medium. Simmer for 8 minutes, and then drain well.

In a large skillet, place a generous spoonful of oil and add the potatoes. Cook for 15 minutes over medium heat, stirring often, or until the potatoes are dry, firm and turning golden brown. Remove the skillet from the heat and set aside.

While the potatoes cook, in a second large skillet, heat a generous spoonful of oil over medium heat. Stir in the onion, pepper, zucchini and celery and cook for 10 minutes, or until the veggies are soft and the onion is translucent. Stir in the tomato, cumin and salt and reduce the heat to medium-low. Cook for 10 minutes to allow the flavors to marry.

Increase the heat to medium and stir in the beef and cilantro. Cook for 7 minutes, stirring often to break up the beef, or until the beef is opaque and cooked through. Stir in the potato before removing the picadillo from the heat. Cover the picadillo to keep it warm while you make the tostones.

To make the tostones, score the unpeeled plantains along their ridged edges with the tip of a sharp knife and then peel them. The peel will be much harder and thicker than a banana peel. Once the plantains are peeled, cut them into ¼" (1.2 cm-) thick slices. Use the flat bottom of a drinking glass to press down on each slice, flattening it and making it thinner.

In a large skillet, heat a generous spoonful of oil over medium heat and add the plantain slices, working in batches so as not to overlap them. Cook them for at least 3 minutes before flipping over each slice. The goal is to have each side be a toasty golden brown. Place the tostones on paper towels and sprinkle them with salt. Serve the picadillo immediately, garnished with a side of tostones.

Coconut Beef Stroganoff with Spaghetti Squash

Makes 4 servings

If you've never had spaghetti squash, you're in for a surprise. It's mind-boggling that running a fork through the cooked squash yields handfuls of pasta-like strands! Unlike pasta, though, spaghetti squash retains a bit of crunch, which is a nice textural contrast to the hearty meat and mushrooms in this recipe. Plus, while the squash roasts, you can use that time to prep the remaining ingredients. The finished stroganoff can rest and gather more flavor while you let the squash cool so that you can comfortably scrape out the strands of squash spaghetti with a fork.

1 spaghetti squash
Coconut oil for cooking
1 yellow onion, chopped
1 pound (448 g) cremini or button mushrooms, sliced
5 cloves garlic, chopped
½ cup (120 ml) dry red wine
2 tablespoons (5 g) thyme
½ teaspoon sea salt
2 teaspoons (12 ml) pomegranate molasses
2 whole anchovies or 1 teaspoon anchovy paste
¾ cup (180 ml) chicken broth
1 tablespoon (7 g) coconut flour
1 pound (448 g) top sirloin, trimmed and cut into ½" (1.2 cm-) thick slices
¼ cup (60 g) Coconut Cream (see page 111)

Preheat the oven to 350°F (180°C) and cover a rimmed baking sheet with aluminum foil or parchment paper.

Halve the squash, trim the ends and scoop out and discard the seeds. (The easiest way to halve spaghetti squash [or any hard winter squash] is to use an 8" [20 cm] chef's knife and a mallet or hammer: Position the knife, dig it into the skin of the squash slightly, and then use the mallet to pound the knife through the squash. Firmly tap one end of the knife and then the other, alternating to create a clean downward cut.)

Place the squash halves on the prepared baking sheet, skin-side up. Pour in just enough water to cover the bottom of the tray, and then bake uncovered for 40 to 60 minutes, or until you can pierce through the flesh with a sharp knife. (If the squash is larger than 2 pounds [896 g], it will probably take 1 hour.) Let cool, and then use a fork to scrape the "spaghetti" strands out of the squash.

While the squash bakes, make the stroganoff. In a large skillet, heat a generous spoonful of oil over medium heat. Stir in the onion and mushrooms and cook, stirring occasionally, for 15 minutes. Stir in the garlic, wine, thyme, salt, molasses and anchovies and continue to cook, stirring occasionally, for another 10 minutes. If you used whole anchovies, mash them to break them up.

Stir in the broth, flour and sirloin and reduce the heat to medium-low. Cook for 5 minutes, occasionally flipping the sirloin strips to cook them evenly, or until the beef has reached the desired doneness. Remove the skillet from the heat and stir in the Coconut Cream, and then gently toss with the spaghetti squash strands.

Leftover stroganoff can be refrigerated for 4 days, and the squash can be refrigerated for 1 week.

Beef Curry with Caramelized Onions, Carrots and Rhubarb

Makes 4 servings

Ever since rhubarb was classified as a fruit by a New York court in 1947, Americans have thought of rhubarb as an ingredient used to make sweet pies, particularly pies involving strawberries. But rhubarb is actually a vegetable. At first glance, it looks like pink celery, and it's perfectly at home in curries and stir-frys. It's tart, it's crunchy and it brings a natural brightness to the table. Just don't eat rhubarb leaves because they contain toxic levels of oxalic acid. But the stalks can be sautéed, simmered or roasted just like any other vegetable. It's time to reclaim rhubarb for our dinner plates!

Coconut oil for cooking
1 sweet onion, thinly sliced
2 large carrots, scrubbed and chopped
1 stalk rhubarb, ends trimmed, stalks chopped
1 red pepper, stem and seeds removed, flesh thinly sliced
¼ small head cabbage, thinly sliced
8 cloves garlic, chopped
3 tablespoons (19 g) curry powder
Dash sea salt
1 pound (448 g) top sirloin, trimmed and cut into ½" (1.2 cm-) thick strips
1 cup (240 ml) whole coconut milk
Handful toasted shelled pumpkin seeds (without shells)

In a large skillet, melt a generous spoonful of oil over medium heat. Add the onion and cook for 20 minutes, stirring often, or until the onion is golden brown and very soft. Note: If you like well-cooked carrots, add the carrots to the onion during the last 10 minutes of their cooking time. Stir in the carrots, rhubarb, pepper, cabbage, garlic, curry powder and salt. Cover the skillet, reduce the heat to medium-low and cook for 10 minutes, stirring once or twice.

Stir in the sirloin and cook, covered, for 3 minutes, flipping the sirloin halfway through. Stir in the milk and pumpkin seeds, re-cover, and cook 3 more minutes, or until sirloin has reached the desired doneness. As with any curry, this dish gathers flavor upon standing, so you don't have to serve this immediately.

Leftover curry can be refrigerated for 4 days.

> **Tip:** *Coconut oil will turn liquid around 78°F (25°C). That doesn't harm the oil.*

Thai Green Papaya Salad with Marinated Lamb

Makes 4 servings

In many Asian cuisines, unripe tropical fruits—particularly papayas and mangos—are often treated like vegetables and served in savory dishes. Likewise, green bananas and plantains are sliced and fried to make chips. It's great to have options! Here's another one: If you really want to get the most out of your papayas, save the faintly peppery-tasting seeds and use them as a garnish. Or you can rinse them well and spread them out on a paper towel to dry. Once they're completely dry, you can grind them with a pepper mill and use them in place of black pepper. Practical meets exotic!

FOR THE MARINADE

1 tablespoon (15 ml) fish sauce
1½ teaspoons (7 ml) pomegranate molasses or tamarind paste
2 tablespoons (30 ml) rice wine vinegar*
Juice of ½ lime
1 clove garlic, minced
Dash crushed red pepper flakes

FOR THE SALAD

½ pound (224 g) green beans, trimmed
½ cup (70 g) raw cashews, chopped
1 red bell pepper, stem and seeds removed, flesh cut into thin slices
3 green onions, green part only, minced
12 cherry tomatoes, cut in half
1 green papaya, peeled and seeds scooped out, flesh cut into ½" (1.2 cm) cubes
Juice of ½ lime
12 large basil leaves
1 sprig mint, leaves only
1 bunch cilantro, leaves only

Coconut oil for cooking
1½ pounds (672 g) leg of lamb, trimmed and cut into ½" (1.2 cm-) thick strips

To make the marinade, in a medium bowl, combine all of the ingredients and mix well. Cover and refrigerate for 4 to 6 hours.

To make the salad, fill a medium pot halfway with water and bring it to a boil. Add the beans and simmer uncovered for 3 minutes. Drain well.

In a medium skillet, toast the cashews over medium heat for 3 minutes, or until they're turning golden brown, shaking the pan often to toast them evenly. Transfer them to a large bowl.

Into the bowl, stir in the pepper, onions, tomatoes, papaya and lime juice.

Place the basil, mint and cilantro on a cutting board and chop them finely, and then mix them into the salad.

In a large skillet, melt a generous dollop of oil over medium heat. Add the lamb and marinade and cook, stirring occasionally, for 5 to 7 minutes, or until the lamb has reached the desired doneness. Use a slotted spoon to transfer the lamb from the skillet to the salad bowl.

Reduce the heat to medium-low and continue to simmer the marinade for 10 minutes. Pour onto the salad and toss well. Serve immediately.

Leftover salad can be refrigerated for 3 days.

*To make this a Paleo-friendly dish, use apple cider vinegar in place of the rice wine vinegar.

Caribbean Taro Empanadas

Makes 12 empanadas

Of all of the members of the root family, taro is the most sticky. In fact, when it's boiled and then mashed, taro almost becomes a paste. Thanks to that incredible stickiness, taro dough can be gently folded and pressed into place almost as readily as wheat-based doughs. Taro roots are the size and shape of a medium beet, but they're hairy and brown. Mash them into poi, make them into dough or incorporate them into your favorite savory pie crust recipe. And keep in mind that brushing doughs and crusts with coconut oil creates a buttery-sweet finish that suits everything from savory dishes to fruit pies.

FOR THE DOUGH

2 pounds (896 g) taro root

2 eggs

½ cup (63 g) corn flour or raw buckwheat flour plus more for dusting*

1 teaspoon sea salt

Coconut oil for brushing

FOR THE FILLING

Coconut oil for cooking and brushing

1 red bell pepper, stem and seeds removed, flesh minced

4 green onions, minced

4 cloves garlic, minced

1 pound (448 g) ground beef

1 tablespoon (7 g) chili powder

1 small bunch cilantro, leaves only, chopped

Preheat the oven to 375°F (190°C) and cover 2 baking sheets with parchment paper.

Bring a medium pot of water to a boil so that you can simmer the taro as soon as it's cut. (It will start to brown immediately!) To prepare the taro, cut each root in half, and then trim away its outer skin, placing it flat-side-down on the cutting board to make trimming the rounded surfaces easier. Cut the inner flesh into rough cubes and simmer for 10 minutes, reducing the heat to medium or even medium-low if they're boiling too furiously. Drain well.

While the taro simmers, make the filling. In a large skillet, melt a generous dollop of oil over medium heat. Stir in the pepper and sauté for about 3 minutes, or until the pepper has begun to soften. Add the onions, garlic, beef, chili powder and cilantro and cook, stirring often to break up the beef, for another 4 minutes, or until the beef is opaque and cooked through. Remove the skillet from the heat.

Place the drained taro in a large bowl and mash it well with a potato masher. Stir in the eggs, flour and salt. Scoop the dough out in ¼ cupfuls (60 ml) and place on the prepared baking sheets, flouring your hands as necessary to prevent the dough from sticking to them. Pat and flatten each scoop into a circle about 5" (13 cm) in diameter, spacing the circles 1" (2.5 cm) apart and again dusting the circles and your hands with flour as necessary. Divide the dough between the 2 baking sheets.

Place a spoonful of filling onto each circle. Working with one empanada at a time, gently fold up one side and tip it back down to form a half-circle or moon shape. Press the edges of the top layer into the edges of the bottom layer to seal it. Gently brush each empanada with melted oil. Bake for 35 minutes, or until the edges of the empanadas are golden brown. Let cool a few minutes before serving. Leftovers can be refrigerated for up to 4 days.

*These flours are not Paleo ingredients, but they are gluten-free and whole-grain.

Vietnamese Coconut Fish Stew

Makes 4 to 6 servings

From sweet-and-sour flavors to adorable baby veggies, this stew has it all. Cod is one of the easiest fish to include because it's typically sold skinless, and it has a hearty texture that stands up to simmering. But any firm-fleshed skinless whitefish will do. Fish cooks quickly, especially when cut into bite-sized cubes, so keep a close eye on the stew once you've added the fish. Shrimp would be equally welcome (and shrimp cook in about 3 minutes), or you could stir in cooked crab during the last few minutes of simmering. If you think you may have leftovers, you could transfer half of the soup to a separate pot, and then add the fish, shrimp or crab to what you'll be serving immediately. Then your leftover "base" soup can serve as a springboard for other ideas.

Coconut oil for cooking
4 green onions, trimmed and minced
6 cloves garlic, minced
1 red bell pepper, seeds and stem removed, flesh thinly sliced
4 cups (32 ounces [948 ml]) vegetable broth
½ cup (93 g) long-grain brown or red rice*
1 cup (240 ml) whole coconut milk
2 tablespoons (30 ml) gluten-free tamari*
1 tablespoon + 1 teaspoon (74 g) pomegranate molasses or tamarind paste
2 teaspoons (4 g) ginger
Pinch cayenne pepper
Juice of 1 lime
4 ounces (112 g) baby corn, drained and roughly chopped
2 heads baby bok choy, ends removed, coarsely chopped
2 tablespoons (3 g) basil
1 pound (448 g) skinless wild Atlantic cod or other skinless firm whitefish, cut into 1″ (2.5 cm) cubes

In a large soup pot, melt the oil over medium heat. Add the onions, garlic and red pepper and cook for 5 minutes, or until the pepper has softened. Stir in the broth, rice, coconut milk, tamari, pomegranate molasses, ginger and cayenne. Reduce the heat to medium-low and simmer, covered, for 40 minutes.

Increase the heat to medium and add the lime juice, corn, bok choy, basil and fish. Cook for 6 minutes, or until the fish is opaque all of the way through. Serve immediately.

Leftover stew can be refrigerated for 3 days.

To make this dish more Paleo-friendly, omit the rice and use coconut aminos in place of the tamari. If you omit the rice, the stew only needs to simmer for 5 minutes—not the 40 minutes needed to cook the rice—before adding the fish.

Curried Triple-Coconut Pea Fritters

Makes about 10 fritters

From stamp-and-go patties in Jamaica to pakoras in India, fritters are a global food. The ingredients differ—stamp-and-go is a fish fritter, whereas pakoras tend to be spicy and made with veggies—but the technique is essentially the same: Mash the ingredients, combine them with enough flour to create patties and then fry them. Coconut oil is great for making fritters because it can handle higher heat, which is what you need when making golden-hued, crispy fritters. They'll be even more crispy and golden brown if you press the fritters into thin patties and flip them very gently so they don't break.

½ cup (43 g) unsweetened flaked coconut, plus more for garnish

Coconut oil for cooking

4 green onions, trimmed and minced

2 cups (about 10 ounces [260 g]) frozen peas, thawed

2 teaspoons (4 g) curry powder

1 teaspoon sea salt

2 eggs

Juice of 1 lime

½ cup (55 g) coconut flour

Coconut Cream for garnishing, optional (see page 111)

In a dry skillet, heat the coconut over medium heat. Cook for 2 to 3 minutes, stirring occasionally, or until the coconut is fragrant and turning golden brown. Transfer the coconut to a food processor.

In a small skillet, melt a dollop of oil over medium-low heat and add the onions. Cook for 4 to 5 minutes, or until the onions are soft and turning golden brown. Add them to the food processor, and then add the peas, curry powder, salt, eggs, lime juice and flour. Process until the peas are mashed and you have a near-paste consistency.

To make the patties, use a ¼ cup (60 ml) measure to scoop out the dough. Firmly press the dough into the measuring cup, and then tap it out into your hand. Gently press the dough into a patty and set it on a large plate or cutting board. Repeat with the remaining dough to make about 10 patties.

In a large skillet, melt a generous dollop of oil over medium heat. Slide the patties into the skillet and press them with a spatula to flatten them a little more. Cook them for 4 minutes, or until the bottoms have browned. Very gently flip the patties over and continue to cook them for another 4 minutes, adding another dollop of oil if the skillet has become dry. Serve immediately, adding a dollop of Coconut Cream, or extra coconut flakes, if you like.

Leftover patties can be refrigerated for 4 days.

Jerk-Rubbed Chicken Rolled with Sun-Dried Tomatoes, Ricotta and Spinach

Makes 4 servings

When you want to pull out a fancy dish to impress guests, meat dishes rolled with colorful veggies never fail to please.

FOR THE JERK
1 tablespoon (6 g) allspice
1 teaspoon ginger
1 teaspoon cinnamon
1 tablespoon (2.7 g) thyme
½ teaspoon sea salt
1 teaspoon freshly ground pepper

FOR THE CHICKEN
Coconut oil for cooking and baking
1 ounce (28 g) sun-dried tomatoes, minced
5 ounces (140 g) curly spinach
1 pound (448 g) chicken breasts, rinsed and patted dry (If you have 2 large breasts rather than 4 smaller ones, butterfly each one and cut them in half lengthwise to create 4 pieces.)
About 5 ounces (140 g) ricotta*

FOR THE SWEET POTATOES
2 sweet potatoes, scrubbed and ends trimmed, cut into 1" (2.5 cm) cubes
1 large onion, chopped
6 cloves garlic, chopped
2 tablespoons (30 ml) red wine vinegar

For a Paleo-friendly dish, omit the ricotta.

Preheat the oven to 350°F (180°C). Place all of the jerk ingredients in a small glass jar and shake well to combine. In an 8"x 8"(20 cm x 20 cm) glass pan, place a dollop of oil and rub the oil onto the bottom and sides of the pan. Set aside.

In a small heatproof bowl, place the tomatoes and cover them with boiling water. Let the tomatoes soak for 20 minutes to soften, and then drain and squeeze dry.

In a large skillet, heat the spinach with a splash of water. Cover and cook on medium heat for about 3 minutes, or until the spinach has wilted, stirring occasionally. Transfer the spinach to a colander, and then run cold water over it to cool it quickly. Use your hands to squeeze as much water out of the spinach as you can.

Place the chicken on a non-porous cutting board—don't use a wooden board because they're harder to clean—and use a mallet to pound the breasts and flatten them slightly. Try to pound each breast into a square-ish shape if you can. Working with one piece at a time, layer each one with spinach, tomatoes and ricotta. Roll each breast and place it seam-side-down in the prepared pan.

Sprinkle each roll of chicken with the jerk seasoning and gently pat the rolls to encourage the jerk to stick. (Reserve the leftover seasoning.) Bake the rolls for 20 minutes, and then remove them from the oven and baste them with the pan juices. Return the rolls to the oven and continue to bake them for another 10 minutes, or until the thickest piece of chicken is opaque when cut in half.

While the chicken bakes, make the sweet potatoes. Fill a large pot halfway with water and bring it to a boil. Add the sweet potatoes and reduce the heat to medium. Simmer the potatoes, covered, for 10 minutes, and then drain.

In a large skillet, melt a dollop of oil over medium heat. Add the onion and cook, stirring occasionally, for 5 minutes, or until the onion is translucent and fragrant. Add the garlic, vinegar and a generous dash of the jerk seasoning. Reduce the heat to medium-low and cook for 3 minutes, or until the garlic is fragrant and softened. Stir in the drained potatoes. Serve the chicken with a side of the sweet potatoes.

Leftover chicken and potatoes can be refrigerated for 3 days.

Cottage Pie

Coconut Oil

Makes 1 deep 9" (23 cm) or 8" x 8" (20 cm x 20 cm) pie

If you've ever been to an Irish pub, you've probably seen Shepherd's Pie on the menu. It's a classic dish; you could call it Irish (and British) comfort food. The difference between Shepherd's Pie and Cottage Pie is that the former contains lamb and the latter contains beef. Aside from that, the seasonings are mostly the same. You'll top this pie with sweet potatoes rather than traditional white potatoes. If you ever want to make Shepherd's Pie, just swap out the beef here for lamb. And perhaps enjoy a cup of Irish or English black tea while you're baking the pie!

Coconut oil for greasing the pan and cooking
2 large sweet potatoes, scrubbed and ends trimmed, cut into 1" (2.5 cm) cubes
5 ounces (140 g) pearl onions (If they're frozen, thaw them first.)
4 large carrots, scrubbed and chopped
4 ribs celery, trimmed and chopped
4 ounces (112 g) frozen peas, thawed
1 pound (448 g) ground beef
2 tablespoons (5 g) thyme
2 tablespoons (3 g) basil
2 teaspoons (2 g) sage
¾ teaspoon sea salt
Freshly ground black pepper
1 cup (240 ml) chicken broth
2 tablespoons (14 g) sweet potato flour or brown rice flour*

Place a large sheet of foil on the lower oven rack. This will prevent any juices from dripping onto the bottom of the oven as the pie cooks. Preheat the oven to 375°F (190°C) and generously grease a deep glass 9" (23 cm) pie dish or an 8" x 8" (20 cm x 20 cm) glass pan with oil.

Fill a large pot halfway with water and bring to a boil. Add the sweet potatoes and reduce the heat to medium. Simmer for 10 minutes, or until you can easily pierce the potatoes with the tip of a knife. Drain the potatoes well, place them back in the dry pot, and use a potato masher to mash the potatoes. Stir in 1 tablespoon (12 g) oil and set aside.

In a large skillet, melt a generous dollop of oil over medium heat. Add the onions, carrots and celery. Cook for 10 minutes, stirring occasionally. Reduce the heat to medium-low and stir in the peas, beef, thyme, basil, sage, salt and pepper. Cook for 2 to 3 minutes, stirring occasionally, or until the beef is lightly browned. Stir in the broth and flour and cook for 2 minutes, stirring often, or until the broth has thickened slightly.

Transfer the meat mixture to the prepared pie dish and top with the mashed sweet potatoes. Bake for 35 to 40 minutes, or until the potatoes are lightly browned on top. Serve piping hot.

Leftover pie can be refrigerated for 5 days.

*For a Paleo-friendly dish, use sweet potato flour.

Recipes with Saturated Fats: Go Ahead and Turn Up the Heat 87

Cardamom-Scented Lentils, Kabocha and Lamb Sauté

Makes 4 servings

Kabocha, or Japanese pumpkin, is a member of the winter squash family. You may have seen it sold as buttercup squash. It's mostly green with orange/yellow blushing, and it looks like an acorn squash that has been smashed by a giant to make it square rather than round. Happily, the non-round character of kabocha means it's much easier to peel and cut into cubes. Just cut the squash into large chunks with an 8˝ (20 cm) chef's knife—use a mallet to pound the knife through the flesh if necessary—and then scoop out the seeds. Trim away the skin before chopping the kabocha into cubes. Its beautiful dark orange flesh gives this sauté a pop of color along with a natural sweetness.

¾ cup (144 g) brown lentils

3 cups (339 g) kabocha or butternut squash, peeled, flesh cut into ½˝ (1.2 cm) cubes

Coconut oil for cooking

1 zucchini, ends trimmed, thinly sliced

2 cups (255 g) peeled pearl onions, thaw if frozen

1½ pounds (672 g) leg of lamb, trimmed and cut into ½˝ (1.2 cm-) thick strips

1 teaspoon cinnamon

½ teaspoon cardamom

2 teaspoons (4 g) coriander

Dash sea salt

Fill a medium pot halfway with water and bring to a boil. Add the lentils and simmer over medium heat for 10 minutes. Add the kabocha and continue to simmer for another 10 minutes, or until the lentils and squash have reached the desired tenderness. Drain well.

In a large skillet, heat a generous spoonful of oil over medium heat. Add the zucchini and onions and cook, stirring occasionally, for 10 minutes, or until the veggies are turning golden brown. Reduce the heat to medium-low and add the lamb, cinnamon, cardamom, coriander and salt. Cook for 8 minutes, or until the lamb is done to your liking. For medium-rare, it should be pink in the center; if you'd like it well done, it should be opaque when cut in half. Stir in the drained lentils and squash and serve immediately.

Leftover sauté can be refrigerated for 4 days.

Coriander-Dusted Lamb Chops with Sautéed Green Beans and Broccoli

Makes 4 servings

When you're shopping for lamb chops (or rack of lamb), you may see cuts that have been "frenched." That just means that the flesh has been trimmed away from the bones to expose them. It's a technique often practiced in French cuisine to give the chops a more elegant look. You can opt for frenched chops if you prefer that look. If you ever roast a frenched rack, though, you might want to cover the bone tips with foil crowns to prevent them from burning. Crowns look like little caps. You'll often see them sold at meat counters.

1 teaspoon coriander
½ teaspoon ginger
½ teaspoon sea salt, plus more for sprinkling
4 lamb chops (totaling about 1½ pounds [672 g]), rinsed and patted dry
¾ pound (336 g) green beans, trimmed
2 heads broccoli, florets only
Coconut oil for cooking
⅓ cup (45 g) roasted macadamia nuts, chopped
6 cloves garlic, cut into thin slices

On a plate, blend the coriander, ginger and salt together. Gently press each side of the lamb into the spice blend, shaking slightly to knock off any excess spice. Set aside.

Rinse the green beans and broccoli and briefly drain them. Transfer them to a large skillet and cook over medium heat for 3 minutes, covered, to steam the veggies. Add a generous spoonful of oil to the veggies and continue to cook, covered, for 5 minutes without disturbing the veggies. Remove them from the heat and toss them with nuts and a sprinkling of salt.

In a large skillet, heat the garlic and a generous spoonful of oil over medium-low heat. Cook for 3 minutes, and then add the lamb. Cook 4 minutes each side—using tongs to flip over the chops—for a total of 8 minutes. Use a spatula to remove the garlic slices from the skillet (place them on small plate), and then cover the skillet and continue to cook the lamb for a final 4 minutes or until the lamb is cooked to the desired doneness. Remove the lamb from the skillet and transfer it to a warm plate. Let the lamb rest 5 minutes before serving. Serve the lamb with the sautéed garlic slices and a side of the green beans and broccoli.

Leftover lamb and veggies can be refrigerated for 4 days.

Caribbean Pumpkin Soup with Tomato, Okra and Chorizo

Makes 4 servings

Looking for a soup that combines the best of all seasons? This pumpkin-based soup has it all: summer (tomatoes and okra), autumn (pumpkin) and winter (kale). Toss in some spices and savory chorizo, and you've got a satisfying soup at any time of the year. Allspice is particularly popular in Caribbean regions, and it is used in both sweet and savory dishes. Contrary to popular misconceptions, "allspice" is not a blend of spices, it's a unique spice that happens to taste like a combination of cinnamon, ginger, cloves and nutmeg—"all of the spices" that were hot commodities when European explorers stumbled upon allspice. The dried allspice berry is sometimes used whole, but more often, it's ground before being stirred into soups, sautés and beverages.

Coconut oil for cooking

1 onion, chopped

½ pound (224 g) cured chorizo, skin removed, cut into small cubes

3 cups (720 ml) chicken broth

1 cup (224 g) canned pumpkin

15 ounces (411 g) canned diced tomatoes

4 ounces (112 g) frozen chopped okra

½ teaspoon allspice

1 teaspoon ginger

2 teaspoons (2 g) thyme

Pinch cayenne pepper

6 kale leaves, tough ribs removed, leaves chopped or roughly torn into small pieces

In a large soup pot, melt a generous spoonful of oil, and then add the onion. Cook for 5 minutes over medium-low heat or just until the onion is turning translucent. Increase the heat to medium, stir in the chorizo and cook for 10 minutes, stirring often.

Stir in the broth, pumpkin and tomatoes and increase the heat to high to bring to a boil. As soon as it boils, reduce the heat to medium and add the okra, allspice, ginger, thyme, pepper and kale. Simmer for 10 minutes, or until the kale has reached the desired tenderness. Serve immediately.

Leftover soup can be refrigerated for 4 days or frozen for 2 months.

Rosemary, Lemon and Garlic Lamb with Roasted Peas, Artichoke Hearts, Red Onions and Carrots

Makes 4 servings

Roasted veggies can be a meal in and of themselves, but they also pair beautifully with meat. And while veggies need a little bit of time to roast, they couldn't be easier to make: just toss them with coconut oil and some sea salt, spread them out on a baking sheet and pop them in the oven. That method works with any vegetable. Just be sure to give each veggie its own quadrant so that you can pull them out of the oven as they shrink and turn golden brown. Smaller veggies will need less roasting time than larger ones do, plus veggies closely sharing a sheet will take longer. But roasting veggies on their own quadrants (or their own individual baking sheets) gives you full culinary control over whatever varieties you choose, and tossing the veggies with coconut oil gives them a faintly sweet and nutty finish. Be creative!

FOR THE VEGGIES

4 carrots, scrubbed and trimmed
Coconut oil for tossing veggies
Dash sea salt
1 red onion, cut into ¼" (0.6 cm-) thick slices
9 ounces (252 g) frozen artichoke hearts, thawed
1 pound (448 g) frozen peas, thawed

FOR THE LAMB

Extra-virgin olive oil
1½ pounds (672 g) leg of lamb, trimmed and cut into ½" (1.2 cm-) thick strips
12 cloves garlic, chopped
3 tablespoons (10 g) dried rosemary
Dash sea salt
Juice of 1 lemon

To roast the veggies, position the oven racks in the upper and lower third of the oven and preheat the oven to 375°F (190°C). Cover 3 baking sheets with parchment paper. If you have a rimmed baking sheet, use that for the peas because they roll. Cut the carrots lengthwise into 4 or 6 long pieces.

In a large bowl, toss the carrots with a dab of coconut oil and a dash of salt. Arrange them on a baking sheet so that none overlap. Repeat with the onion, artichoke and peas, making sure to give each veggie its own quadrant on the baking sheet.

Roast the carrots and peas for 30 minutes, and then remove them from the oven. Allow the artichoke hearts and red onions to roast for another 10 minutes. Remove them from the oven. If you want extra-crisp onions, flip over the onion slices and return them to the oven for a final 10 minutes.

During the final 10 minutes of roasting, make the lamb. Pour a drizzle of olive oil into a large skillet over medium-low heat, then add the lamb. As soon as it starts to brown—it'll only take a minute or two—add the garlic and rosemary. Cook for 5 minutes, flipping pieces over halfway through. Add the salt and lemon juice and continue to cook for 3 minutes or until the lamb is done to your liking. For medium-rare, it should be pink in the center; if you'd like it well done, it should be opaque when cut in half. Serve immediately with a side of roasted veggies.

Leftover lamb and veggies can be refrigerated for 4 days.

Ham, Cauliflower and Sweet Potato Hash

Makes 4 hearty servings

Thanks to the oregano, ham and onion in this hash, it has a pizza-flavored flair. (Feel free to top the hash with shredded mozzarella cheese to complete that impression.) Thanks to its savory heartiness, hash is welcome any time of day, from morning to night. Steaming the sweet potatoes before sautéing them in the same skillet saves on time and cleanup, or you could use leftover already-cooked potatoes to get your hash on the table even faster. Try serving leftover hash topped with freshly poached eggs for an almost-instant breakfast.

1 head cauliflower, florets only

1½ pounds (672 g) sweet potatoes, scrubbed and trimmed, cut into ½" (1.2 cm) cubes

¼ cup (60 ml) water

Coconut oil for cooking

1 large yellow onion, chopped

4 cloves garlic, chopped

2 tablespoons (6 g) oregano

1 pound (448 g) ham, cut into ½" (1.2 cm) cubes

Sea salt to taste

Fill a large pot halfway with water and bring to a boil. Add the cauliflower and reduce the heat to medium. Simmer, covered, for 5 minutes, and then drain.

In a large skillet, heat the sweet potatoes and water over medium-high heat, covered, for 5 minutes, or until you can comfortably cut a potato cube in half with the edge of a spatula. You should encounter a little resistance—you don't want the potatoes to be mushy—but the edge of a spatula should be able to go through the potato fairly easily. If any water remains in the skillet, drain the potatoes, and then return them to the skillet.

Add a generous spoonful of oil and the onion to the skillet. Cook the potatoes and onion over medium heat for 10 minutes, or until the potatoes are turning golden brown. Add the garlic, drained cauliflower and oregano and continue cooking another 5 minutes over medium-low heat. During the final minute of cooking, stir the in ham to warm it through. Add salt to taste and serve immediately.

Leftover hash can be refrigerated for 4 days.

Pork Burgers with Cilantro-Papaya Ketchup with Mashed Yuca

Makes 4 servings

You may not have heard of yuca, but you've probably already eaten it. The same plant is called "tapioca" in the United States, "cassava" in African countries and "manioc" in Brazil. Be sure to completely trim away the outer "bark" and the underlying purple-tinged tough fibers before you cut the yuca into cubes. Yuca tastes like a lighter, sweeter version of potatoes, which makes the yuca a great pair for flavorful ketchup and garlic-accented pork burgers.

FOR THE KETCHUP

1 red bell pepper
Coconut oil for cooking
1 large onion, chopped
4 cloves garlic, chopped
1 cup (175 g) chopped papaya (about 1 medium Hawaiian papaya), plus more for garnishing
3 tablespoons (45 ml) cider vinegar
1½ teaspoons (4 g) ground dry mustard
½ teaspoon allspice
½ teaspoon ginger
½ teaspoon sea salt
½ bunch cilantro, leaves only, chopped, plus some whole leaves for garnishing

FOR THE YUCA

1½ pounds (672 g) yuca, outer "bark" cut away and ends trimmed, flesh cut into 1" (2.5 cm) cubes
Coconut oil for mashing
Sea salt to taste

FOR THE BURGERS

1 pound (448 g) ground pork
2 cloves garlic, minced
6 green onions, trimmed and minced
Generous dash sea salt
Generous dash freshly ground black pepper
Coconut oil for cooking

First, roast the pepper: Place a piece of foil on a rimmed baking sheet and position it in the center of the middle oven rack, and then place the whole pepper directly on the oven rack over the sheet. The sheet will catch the drips. Roast the pepper for at least 20 minutes at 450°F (230°C). When the pepper's skin is blistered and blackening, remove and let it cool. Then peel away the skin and discard the stem and seeds. No need to chop the pepper.

While the pepper roasts, in a medium skillet, heat a dab of oil over medium heat and add the onion. Cook, stirring occasionally, for 5 minutes, or until the onion is turning translucent. Add the garlic and continue to cook for another 3 minutes, or until the garlic is fragrant. If the roasted pepper is ready, add it to the skillet; if not, remove the skillet from heat until the pepper is ready. Stir in the pepper and the remaining ketchup ingredients except the cilantro and simmer over medium-low heat for 10 minutes, stirring occasionally to break up the papaya and pepper. Stir in the cilantro and cook for a final 5 minutes before removing the skillet from the heat. Transfer the mixture to a food processor and blend for a few seconds, just until you have a chunky ketchup. Set aside.

Fill a medium pot halfway with water and bring it to a boil. Add the yuca and simmer uncovered over medium heat for 15 minutes, or until you can easily pierce the yuca with the tip of a knife. Drain the yuca well, and then place it in a pot and mash with a generous spoonful of oil and a dash of salt. Cover the yuca to keep it warm.

While the yuca simmers, make the burgers. In a large bowl, combine the pork, garlic and onions, using your hands to mix well. Form the mixture into 4 equal patties. Season the patties with salt and pepper. In a large skillet, heat a dab of oil over medium-low heat and add the patties. Cook for 3 minutes, or until the patties are browned, and then flip and continue to cook—slightly flattening the patties with a spatula—for another 2 to 3 minutes, or until both sides are browned and the patties are cooked through. Serve the patties with the ketchup and a side of the mashed yuca, garnishing the plate with extra chopped papaya and whole cilantro leaves.

Nutty Sugar Snap Pea, Chicken and Cucumber Stir-Fry with Clementines

Makes 4 servings

Sugar snap peas, snow peas and green beans are uncommon in the world of legumes because they have edible pods that house very immature, easily digested beans. It's easy to see the difference between sugar snap and snow peas, though: the former is rounded and bulky, while the latter is flat. They're both delicious raw—that's when they're at their most crunchy—but they work well in stir-frys, too. Just don't cook them for more than 8 to 10 minutes if you want the pods to still have some snap. And as you're rinsing the sugar snap peas, you may want to snap off the stem end and peel away the two strings on either side (they look like seams) if they look especially tough or fibrous. That way, you'll wind up with crisp-but-tender-in-the-right-places pods.

Coconut oil for cooking

4 medium carrots, scrubbed and chopped

1 large onion, chopped

½ English cucumber, chopped

1 pound (448 g) chicken breast, trimmed and cut into bite-sized pieces

½ pound (224 g) sugar snap peas, any tough strings peeled away and discarded

6 cloves garlic, chopped

2 clementines or tangerines, peeled and gently separated into segments

¼ cup (64 g) cashew butter

1 to 2 tablespoons (15 to 30 ml) gluten-free tamari, depending on how salty you want your dish to be*

2 teaspoons (4 g) ginger

4 eggs, lightly whisked with a fork

In a large skillet, melt a generous dab of oil over medium heat. Add the carrots, onion and cucumber and cook for 5 minutes, stirring occasionally, or until the onion is fragrant. Add the chicken, peas and garlic and cook another 5 minutes, or until the garlic is fragrant and the thickest piece of chicken is opaque when cut in half.

Stir in the clementines, cashew butter, tamari and ginger and reduce the heat to medium-low. Stir well to combine. Add the eggs and gently stir them into the veggies and chicken to scramble them. The eggs should cook through in about 2 minutes. Serve immediately.

Leftover stir-fry can be refrigerated for 3 days.

*For a Paleo-friendly dish, use coconut aminos in place of the tamari.

Gingered Sweet Potato Bisque with Lamb and Spinach

Makes 4 servings

Bisques are usually thickened with cream, but this time, you'll be mashing sweet potatoes and then stirring them into the soup to make a smooth base for the savory lamb, turnips and spinach. Try to find garnet-hued sweet potatoes. They're red rather than orange, and that beautiful rich color makes for a gorgeous soup. Or for a truly eye-catching dish, use purple sweet potatoes! They're amethyst purple on the outside and a brilliant indigo on the inside. Their presence makes any dish look stunning, not to mention unforgettably exotic.

2 large sweet potatoes, scrubbed and cut into 1" (2.5 cm) cubes
Coconut oil for cooking
1 yellow onion, chopped
4 carrots, scrubbed and chopped
1 pound (448 g) ground lamb
4 cups (960 ml) chicken broth
2 large turnips, peeled and cut into bite-sized pieces
½ teaspoon sea salt (or more to taste)
10 ounces (280 g) curly spinach, coarsely chopped
2" (5 cm) fresh ginger root, peeled and minced or pressed with a garlic press
Coconut Cream for garnishing, optional (see page 111)

Fill a large pot halfway with water and bring to a boil. Add the sweet potatoes and reduce the heat to medium. Simmer uncovered for 10 minutes, and then drain. Place the potatoes back into the dry pot and mash them with a potato masher. Set aside.

While the sweet potatoes cook, in a large soup pot, heat a generous dollop of oil over medium heat. Add the onion and carrots and cook, stirring occasionally, for 5 minutes, or until the onion is turning translucent. Stir in the lamb, using the edge of a spatula to break it up. Cook just until the lamb is beginning to brown.

Pour in the broth and bring it to a boil over high heat. Add the turnips and reduce the heat to medium-low. Simmer for 8 minutes, and then stir in the salt, spinach and ginger. Cook, stirring often, for 2 minutes to wilt the spinach.

Remove the bisque from the heat and stir in the mashed sweet potatoes to create a thick bisque effect. Serve promptly, garnishing with the Coconut Cream if you'd like a creamier texture.

Leftover bisque can be refrigerated for 4 days.

Beef and Quinoa Lettuce Tacos with Fried Avocado

Makes 4 servings

Who says you need corn tortillas to make tacos? Sturdy Romaine leaves work just as well, plus they provide a tooth-friendly crunch. That crunch pairs perfectly with hearty beef, quinoa and creamy fried avocado. Yes, fried avocado—yet another way to enjoy nature's lushest fruit! If you want more avocado with your tacos, buy an extra one to make Guacamole (see page 152.) Avocados make any dish more sublime and satisfying.

FOR THE TACOS

¼ cup (43 g) quinoa*

¾ cup (180 ml) water

2 tablespoons (30 ml) melted coconut oil, divided

2 large avocados, peeled, pits removed, flesh cut into ½" (1.2 cm) cubes

1 yellow onion, chopped

1 red bell pepper, stem and seeds removed, flesh cut into thin strips

1 pound (448 g) ground beef

4 cloves garlic, chopped

2 tablespoons (15 g) chili powder

2 teaspoons (5 g) cumin

8 large Romaine leaves, rinsed and patted dry

OPTIONAL GARNISHES

Whole-milk plain Greek yogurt**

Salsa

Chopped fresh cilantro

Lime wedges

In a medium skillet, bring the quinoa and water to a boil. Reduce the heat to a simmer, cover and cook on low for 15 minutes, or until the quinoa has reached the desired tenderness and its hulls have begun to uncurl into enchanting spirals. Drain (if needed) and set aside.

While the quinoa simmers, in a medium skillet, heat 1 tablespoon (15 ml) of the oil and the avocados over medium-low heat. Cook for 10 to 12 minutes, occasionally flipping the avocado cubes to brown them evenly on all sides. Slide the browned avocados onto a cool plate.

In a large skillet, heat the remaining 1 tablespoon (15 ml) oil. Stir in the onion and pepper and cook over medium heat for 8 minutes, or until the onion has started to soften and turn translucent. Stir in the beef, garlic, chili powder and cumin and continue to cook, stirring often, for another 4 minutes, or until the beef is cooked through. Stir in the cooked quinoa.

Fill each Romaine leaf with the taco mixture and top with the fried avocado. Serve with the optional garnishes.

Leftover taco mixture can be refrigerated for 3 days.

Quinoa isn't a Paleo ingredient, but it is gluten-free and whole-grain.

**For a Paleo-friendly dish, omit the yogurt.*

Tangerine Chicken with Cauliflower Steaks

Makes 4 servings

For decades, General Tso's chicken has been on the menu in Chinese restaurants. This version is an upgrade: You'll use naturally sweet tangerines instead of white sugar, and you'll thicken the sauce with coconut flour, not cornstarch. Toss in some spices, a tangy kick from apple cider vinegar, and you've got the makings of a newly re-created classic!

FOR THE CAULIFLOWER STEAKS

1 head cauliflower, rinsed
Coconut oil for cooking and roasting
½ teaspoon sea salt

FOR THE CHICKEN

3 tablespoons (20 g) coconut flour
Pinch cloves
Pinch cinnamon
Pinch cayenne pepper
Freshly ground black pepper
4 tangerines
2 pounds (896 g) chicken thighs, trimmed and cut into oversized bite-sized pieces
½ cup (70 g) cashews
2 tablespoons (24 g) coconut oil plus more if needed
1 yellow onion, chopped
3 cloves garlic, minced
2 tablespoons (30 ml) gluten-free tamari*
3 tablespoons (45 ml) apple cider vinegar
Toasted sesame oil for garnishing

*For a Paleo-friendly dish, use coconut aminos in place of the tamari.

Preheat the oven to 400°F (200°C) and cover a baking sheet with parchment paper.

Strip away the bottom leaves from the cauliflower. Cut the head in half, starting with the top of the head and cutting through to the base. Cut the head into "steaks" about ½" (1.2 cm) wide, starting at the center and slicing toward the outer edge of the florets. Depending on how thick the main "branch" is at the base of the head, you'll get 4 to 6 steaks. Save the outer florets that fall away.

In a large skillet, melt a knob of oil over medium heat. Cook the cauliflower steaks for 2 to 3 minutes per side, or until both sides are browned, working in batches if necessary. Repeat with the loose cauliflower florets, browning them as well. Transfer the steaks and florets to the prepared baking sheet, sprinkle with salt and roast for 25 minutes, or until tender.

While the cauliflower roasts, make the chicken. In a medium mixing bowl, combine the flour, spices and the zest of 2 tangerines. Add the chicken and toss to coat well. Set aside.

In a large skillet, toast the cashews over medium heat for 3 minutes, or until they're turning golden brown, shaking the pan often to toast them evenly. Transfer the cashews to a cool plate. In the same skillet, melt the 2 tablespoons (24 g) coconut oil. Add the chicken, reserving any dredging that falls off the chicken pieces. Cook the chicken for 7 minutes, or until cooked through and golden brown, occasionally flipping to cook all sides. Remove the chicken to a plate.

In the same skillet, cook the onion over medium heat for 3 minutes, adding more oil if the skillet becomes too dry. Stir in the garlic and continue to cook for 2 minutes, or until the onion and garlic are soft and fragrant. Stir in the juice of 2 tangerines and the sections of 2 tangerines, the tamari, vinegar and the reserved dredging mixture.

Cook for 3 minutes, stirring often. Reduce the heat to medium-low and add the chicken and toasted cashews. Heat through for 2 minutes. Right before removing the chicken from the skillet, stir in a drizzle of toasted sesame oil. Serve immediately with the cauliflower steaks and florets.

Baked Cinnamon Apples
with Almond, Coconut and Date Streusel

Makes 4 servings (one-half apple each)

Typical streusel is made with white flour, white sugar and butter. Rather than the usual Big Three of the streusel world, though, this recipe includes almond flour and flaked coconut in place of flour, dates instead of white sugar and coconut oil in lieu of butter. Butter works well, too, but coconut oil is softer and easier to cut into crumbs with a pastry cutter. (Coconut oil that's stored above 78°F [25°C] will be liquid. Just stir it in.) If you like, you can garnish the baked apples with a dollop of mascarpone to add a creamy richness. Mascarpone is thickened cream with little or no lactose-containing whey remaining in it, which makes mascarpone incredibly lush and very low in sugar. If you ever want an instant frosting—perhaps for your apples?—just stir a hint of vanilla and a drizzle of maple syrup into a small tub of mascarpone. It's so easy, and sooooo tasty.

¼ cup (23 g) almond flour
¼ cup (21 g) flaked unsweetened coconut
1 teaspoon cinnamon
½ teaspoon allspice
¼ teaspoon cloves
4 dates, pitted and minced
1 teaspoon vanilla
2 large, firm apples, such as Pink Lady or Gala
2 tablespoons (24 g) coconut oil, chilled
½ cup (120 ml) cider or water
Mascarpone cheese for serving*

Preheat the oven to 350°F (180°C) and have an 8"x 8" (20 cm x 20 cm) glass baking dish ready.

In a medium bowl, mix the flour, coconut, cinnamon, allspice, cloves, dates and vanilla together.

Halve the apples and cut away the stems. Trim a little off of each "bottom" to create a level surface so that the apples don't roll around in the dish. Use a spoon to scoop out the cores, and then arrange the apples in the baking dish.

Add the oil to the streusel mix and use a pastry cutter to cut the mix into coarse crumbs. Fill the apple halves with the streusel and pour the cider into the bottom of the baking dish.

Tightly cover the baking dish with foil or a heat-safe lid. Bake for 20 minutes, and then uncover and continue to bake for another 15 minutes, or until the apples have reached the desired tenderness. Serve the apples warm with a dollop of mascarpone.

Leftover apples can be refrigerated for 5 days.

For a Paleo-friendly dish, omit the mascarpone.

Coconut Banana Cream Pie

Makes 1 (9" [23 cm]) pie

This sweet and creamy pie will make you think of Bananas Foster, the classic dessert made with caramelized bananas and whipped cream. This version, though, is done raw-dessert style, with a crust made of nuts, coconut and dates. But the interior is cooked to give the bananas a lusher flavor. Be sure to allow time for the coconut milk to thicken in the fridge before you serve the pie. If you rush the setting process, your pie will seem more like melting ice cream atop crust. Also, use whole coconut milk. "Light" coconut milk, which is essentially watered-down coconut milk, doesn't contain enough fat to thicken when chilled.

FOR THE CRUST

1 cup (100 g) walnut halves
½ cup (40 g) gluten-free rolled oats*
1 cup (85 g) unsweetened coconut flakes
4 dates, pitted
2 tablespoons (30 ml) melted coconut oil plus more if needed

FOR THE PIE FILLING

2 ripe bananas
1 tablespoon + ¼ cup (75 ml) melted coconut oil, divided
1 teaspoon vanilla
Pinch sea salt
15 ounces (440 ml) canned whole coconut milk, unshaken and chilled in the refrigerator for at least 6 hours

Tip: Need to grease a pan? Use saturated fats because they can handle higher heat.

In a large skillet, toast the walnuts and oats over medium heat, shaking the pan occasionally, for 3 minutes. Add the coconut and continue to toast for another 2 minutes, or until everything is fragrant and turning light brown. Immediately transfer the mixture to a food processor. Add the dates and oil and process until the crust starts to clump together. (Add another tablespoon [15 ml] oil if it's not clumping.) Press into a 9" (23 cm) pie pan.

Peel and slice the bananas and place them in the same skillet you used for toasting the nuts and oats. Add 1 tablespoon (15 ml) of the oil. Sauté the bananas over medium heat for 3 to 5 minutes, or until they've begun to caramelize, flipping them about halfway through. Transfer the bananas to a food processor and add the remaining ¼ cup (60 ml) oil and the vanilla and salt.

To make Coconut Cream: After the can has chilled for 6 hours, carefully open it and scoop off the cream that has risen to the top. It's extremely important to use well-chilled, unshaken whole coconut milk because warm or shaken whole coconut milk will be homogeneous and therefore too thin. Chilling whole coconut milk causes the cream to separate and rise to the top.

Add the cream to the food processor with the bananas and blend until the filling is smooth. Pour the filling into the crust and refrigerate for at least 3 hours to fully set the pie before you serve it.

Pie can be refrigerated for up to 1 week, although the cooked bananas will cause the pie to become faintly brownish-purple after a few hours. Don't worry about that; it tastes just as delicious. If you like, toast extra coconut flakes and scatter them on top as an attractive (and distracting) garnish.

Gluten-free oats are not a Paleo ingredient, but they are whole-grain and gluten-free.

Chai-Spiced Coconut Pudding with Deep-Fried Coconut Flakes

Makes four 4-ounce (120 ml) ramekins

You've probably had chai tea with breakfast, but how about as a dessert? This recipe combines the warm spiciness of chai with rich, lightly sweet coconut milk to create an easy custard. If you'd like to get especially creative, you can make your own chai blend by combining 1 teaspoon of black tea with 2 whole cardamom pods, 4 whole cloves, 1 small cinnamon stick, several black peppercorns and a small piece of fresh ginger root. Place them all in a teabag, or bundle them in a square of cheesecloth and tie it shut with a cotton string, and then gently smash the bag with the bottom of a drinking glass to release the spicy flavors before adding the bag to the coconut milk. You may like your own chai combination so much that you'll want to make DIY chai your new morning ritual!

15 ounces (440 ml) whole unsweetened coconut milk
3 tablespoons (45 ml) melted coconut oil, divided
¼ cup (60 ml) maple syrup
1 bag chai tea or homemade
¼ cup (21 g) unsweetened flaked coconut
2 eggs
1 teaspoon vanilla

Set out four 4-ounce (120 ml) ramekins.

In a medium pot, place the milk, 2 tablespoons (30 ml) of the oil, the maple syrup and tea over medium heat. Simmer for 10 minutes, whisking often, to allow the tea to infuse into the milk.

While the coconut mixture simmers, in a small skillet, heat the remaining 1 tablespoon (15 ml) oil over medium heat. Add the coconut and cook for 1 to 2 minutes, or until the flakes are turning golden brown. Quickly remove the flakes from the heat and spread them out on a paper towel to dry.

In a medium bowl, crack the eggs and whisk well. As soon as the coconut mixture has simmered for 10 minutes, remove the tea bag from the mixture and discard it. With a heatproof cup or spoon, gradually whisk about half of the coconut mixture into the eggs. Reduce the heat to the lowest setting, or turn off the heat entirely if you're using an electric stove; you'll have plenty of residual heat, and gradually whisk the egg mixture back into the coconut mixture, whisking constantly for 1 minute. The pudding will thicken almost instantly. Quickly remove the pot from the heat, add the vanilla and pour the custard into the waiting ramekins.

Allow the puddings to cool on a wire rack for 10 minutes before topping them with the fried coconut flakes. If you'd like more of a custard effect, chill the puddings for 1 hour before serving them. Refrigerate the pudding for up to 4 days.

Almost-Raw Chocolate Orange Pie with Coconut Crust

Makes 1 (9" [23 cm]) pie

This hybrid pie combines the typical ingredients and methods used in making raw desserts with a flavor-concentrating cooking technique. Aside from a little simmering and melting time, though, making this pie is as easy as flipping the food processor switch to the "on" position. You won't even have to wash the processor between making the crust and the filling. Just remember to make the pie ahead of time so that it has at least six hours to chill before you serve it. (The coconut oil will help the pie set as it chills.) If you're going to freeze the pie, you might want to pre-cut it—after the initial chill, of course—to make it easier to remove individual slices later.

FOR THE FILLING
4 navel oranges, juice and zest
4 avocados, peeled and pitted
¼ cup (16 g) unsweetened cocoa powder, preferably un–Dutched
¼ cup (60 ml) maple syrup
2 ounces (58 g) 85 percent chocolate
¼ cup (60 ml) melted coconut oil

FOR THE CRUST
½ cup (55 g) sliced almonds
1 cup (100 g) pecans
1 cup (85 g) unsweetened coconut flakes
8 dates, pitted
1 teaspoon vanilla
Dash sea salt

Use a microplane or zester to zest the oranges, catching the zest in a large bowl. Place the freshly squeezed orange juice in a small pot along with the zest. Bring to a boil, and then reduce the heat to low and simmer for 45 minutes.

Meanwhile, place all of the crust ingredients in a food processor and process until you have moist crumbs. Press the crust into a glass 9" (23 cm) pie pan and refrigerate it.

To complete the filling, place the simmered and reduced orange juice and zest in the food processor along with the avocados, cocoa powder and maple syrup.

Break the chocolate into chunks and place them in a small pot along with the oil. Heat on the lowest setting to allow the chocolate to gently and slowly melt. Stir often and remove the pan from the heat when there are still a few lumps in the chocolate. Finish melting the chocolate by gently swirling the pan.

Add the chocolate mixture to the food processor and process until you have a smooth filling. Spoon into the crust and refrigerate for at least 6 hours before serving.

The pie can be refrigerated for 1 week or frozen for 3 months.

Chocolate-Dipped Fruit and Nut Balls

Makes about 20 balls

Have an urge to play with your food? These chocolate-coated nut balls are fun to make, plus you'll have a chance to practice your chopstick skills. You could use a fork to dip the balls into the melted chocolate, but chopsticks are less messy, and they make it easier to completely coat each ball and maneuver it from the pot to the plate. (If you use a fork, don't stab into the balls. Just rest each ball on the tines and then dip it.) Or if you'd rather enjoy these nut balls as a to-go snack, omit the chocolate and simply roll the fruit and nut mixture into balls. Then you'll have a non-meltable treat you can tuck into a bag when you leave the house.

6 pitted dates, finely chopped

½ cup (130 g) nut butter (almond and/or peanut work best), chilled

¾ cup (64 g) unsweetened flaked coconut

2 tablespoons (40 g) honey

½ cup (69 g) roasted pumpkin seeds, twirled in a food processor until they're coarsely ground

1 tablespoon (15 ml) melted coconut oil

3½ ounces (100 g) 85 percent dark chocolate

In a large mixing bowl, mix all of the ingredients except the chocolate. For finer-textured balls, run the ingredients (sans chocolate) through a food processor. Shape the nut mixture into 1" (2.5 cm) balls, place them in a single layer on a rimmed baking sheet and refrigerate them for at least 1 hour to chill them thoroughly.

Meanwhile, break the chocolate into chunks and place them in a small pot. Heat on the lowest setting to allow the chocolate to gently and slowly melt. Stir often and remove the pan from the heat when there are still a few lumps in the chocolate. Finish melting the chocolate by gently swirling the pan.

Cover a large plate with parchment paper. Using a pair of chopsticks, dip each nut ball into the chocolate and place it on the covered plate. The chilled nut balls will cause the chocolate to harden quickly, and the parchment paper will make it easy to pop the nut balls free as soon as the chocolate is set. If necessary, just peel the paper away from the balls.

Keep the chocolate-covered nut balls refrigerated to prevent the chocolate from melting. These snacks will last in the refrigerator for 1 week—if you can manage to keep them around that long! Or you can freeze them for up to 1 month.

Ethiopian-Style Collards and Onions

Makes 4 side servings, plus extra berbere spice mix to use in other dishes

The Ethiopian spice blend called berbere is intoxicating. It's fabulous on everything from popcorn to steak to broccoli. The only unusual spice in the mix is fenugreek, which tastes rather like celery salt. Fenugreek is more earthy and creamy than celery salt, though, and it's well worth seeking out. You might like to try toasting whole fenugreek seeds and grinding them yourself for maximum flavor. If you like your food spicy, add more cayenne pepper to the blend. (Some berbere blends are based on cayenne rather than sweet paprika.) The contrast of "sweet" spices such as cinnamon and cloves with "savory" spices including pepper and fenugreek makes this blend so enchanting.

FOR THE BERBERE SPICE MIX

1 tablespoon (7 g) sweet paprika
½ teaspoon fenugreek
¾ teaspoon sea salt
¼ teaspoon ginger
⅛ teaspoon cardamom
¼ teaspoon nutmeg
⅛ teaspoon allspice
⅛ teaspoon cloves
⅛ teaspoon cinnamon
Dash cayenne pepper

FOR THE COLLARDS

1 bunch collards
Ghee for cooking
1 large yellow onion, chopped
5 cloves garlic, sliced
1 tablespoon (7 g) berbere spice mix (see above)

In a clean spice jar, place all of the berbere ingredients and shake well to combine. (If you don't have one of the spices in the list, it's okay to omit it.)

Sort through the collard leaves and discard any that are yellow. Rinse the leaves well and whack them a few times against the side of the sink to dry them. Rip away and discard the tough stems. Roll the leaves into tight tubes, and then slice them to create long ribbons.

In a large skillet, melt a dollop of ghee over medium heat. Add the onion and cook for 5 minutes, stirring occasionally. Stir in the collards, cover and cook for 5 minutes undisturbed. Uncover and stir in the garlic and berbere spice mix.

Reduce the heat to medium-low and cook uncovered, stirring occasionally, for 8 to 10 minutes, or until the collard ribbons have wilted and the garlic has softened. Serve immediately.

Leftover collards can be refrigerated for 4 days. They make a particularly nice breakfast when topped with a poached egg!

Coffee-Rubbed Bison with Roasted Roots

Makes 4 servings

The rich flavor of ghee makes it an ideal partner for bison, while the faint sweetness of coconut oil complements the natural sweetness of roasted roots. If you don't have ghee on hand, you can use butter instead. That's true for any recipe calling for ghee. Just remember that when you use butter in any recipe, don't heat it past medium or medium-high. Ghee is what you need for high-heat cooking. Because you'll be using bison in this recipe, you want to keep the heat around medium to avoid overcooking the meat. But you might as well use ghee anyway to take advantage of its exceptionally full flavor. It tastes more buttery than butter!

FOR THE BISON

2 teaspoons (5 g) chili powder

2 teaspoons (2 g) finely ground coffee

1 pound (448 g) trimmed bison steaks, rinsed and patted dry

Ghee for cooking

Balsamic vinegar for deglazing (optional)

FOR THE ROOTS

2 sweet potatoes, scrubbed but not peeled, cut into 1" (2.5 cm) cubes

About ¾ teaspoon sea salt, divided

About 1 tablespoon (15 ml) warmed coconut oil, divided

4 parsley roots or parsnips, green tops removed, roots scrubbed and cut in half

12 radishes, scrubbed and quartered

In a small bowl, mix the chili powder with the coffee. Place the steaks on a non-porous cutting board—not wood because they are more difficult to clean—sprinkle on the chili powder mixture and gently press the mixture into the steaks. Cover the steaks and refrigerate them for at least 6 hours or overnight.

Preheat the oven to 375°F (190°C). Line 2 baking sheets with parchment paper.

In a large bowl, toss the sweet potatoes with ¼ teaspoon of the salt and 1 teaspoon of the oil. Arrange the potatoes on a baking sheet so that none overlap. Repeat with the parsley roots and radishes, tossing each with ¼ teaspoon of salt and 1 teaspoon of oil and then arranging them on the second baking sheet. Roast the veggies for 30 minutes.

While the roots roast, finish the steaks. In a nonstick skillet, melt a knob of ghee over medium heat, and then add the steaks and cook for 4 minutes. Flip the steaks, cover and reduce the heat to medium-low. Cook for another 4 minutes for medium-rare steaks or 6 minutes for medium-well, cutting into the thickest part of the steaks to test doneness before transferring the steaks to a warm plate.

If you like, add a dash of vinegar to the skillet, and then gently loosen the drippings on the bottom of the skillet, deglazing it to create a rich "zip" sauce. Serve the steaks with a drizzle of the zip sauce (if using) and a side of the roasted roots.

Leftover steaks can be refrigerated for 3 days; leftover roots can be refrigerated for 5 days.

Tip: *You can rub the steaks with the mix and cook them right away, but to capture the most flavor from the rub, it's best to refrigerate the rubbed meat for at least 6 hours.*

Moroccan Harira with Lamb and Lentils

Makes 4 to 6 servings

This thick, hearty stew is traditionally served to break the fast during Ramadan. But even if you haven't been fasting from sunrise to sunset, harira is an intoxicating blend of flavors. Sweet spices such as cinnamon and ginger lend the savory lamb a distinctly North African flavor, and the lemons contribute their unique brightness to the mix. To make the stew even richer, you'll stir an egg into it to finish it off. It only takes a minute or two to cook the egg, and much like Greek egg lemon soup, the yolk will thicken the broth while the white forms pretty ribbons. Finishing touches don't get much easier than that!

Ghee for cooking
1 large onion, chopped
2 large carrots, scrubbed and chopped
1 pound (448 g) ground lamb
4 cups (32 ounces [960 ml]) chicken or vegetable broth
½ cup (93 g) long-grain brown rice*
2 teaspoons (4 g) ginger
1 teaspoon cinnamon
2 teaspoons (5 g) cumin
1 tablespoon (7 g) turmeric
Dash cayenne pepper
Dash sea salt
½ cup (96 g) brown lentils*
3 large tomatoes, chopped
1 can (15 ounces or [425 g]) chickpeas, undrained*
Juice of ½ lemon
1 egg
Small bunch cilantro, leaves only

In a large soup pot, melt a knob of ghee over medium heat. Add the onion and carrots and cook, stirring occasionally, for 6 minutes, or until the onion is turning golden brown. Stir in the lamb. Cook for 3 minutes, or until the lamb is cooked through, stirring often to break up the lamb.

Stir in the broth, rice, ginger, cinnamon, cumin, turmeric, cayenne and salt. Increase the heat to high. As soon as the soup reaches a boil, reduce the heat to low and simmer, covered, for 25 minutes. Increase the heat to medium-low and stir in the lentils, tomatoes and chickpeas. Cook, uncovered, for another 25 minutes, or until the rice and lentils have reached the desired tenderness.

Reduce the heat to low and stir in the lemon juice, egg and cilantro, stirring constantly for a minute or two. The egg will cook almost instantly, and it will form pretty white swirls in the soup. Remove from the heat and serve immediately.

Leftover harira can be refrigerated for 5 days or frozen for 3 months. Like all tomato-based soups and sauces, harira becomes even more delicious upon standing. It also thickens quite a bit, so you might want to stir in some extra broth when reheating it.

To make this a Paleo-friendly dish, replace the rice with chopped raw cauliflower florets, stirred in during the last 5 minutes of cooking. Likewise, omit the lentils and chickpeas and instead stir in chopped green beans along with the cauliflower.

Potatoes Paprikash with Scrambled Eggs

Makes 4 servings

In American cookery, caraway seeds are pretty much used as decorations. Bakers sometimes sprinkle them onto bagels and loaves along with poppy seeds and salt crystals. In northern and central European countries, though, caraway is an essential ingredient in everything from rye bread to traditional holiday cookies. It also makes an appearance in soups, stews and savory dishes like this paprikash. Ever had caraway cheese? Delicious. Ditto for sauerkraut made with caraway. Caraway is also grown in northern African and Middle Eastern countries, where it's a popular addition to puddings and spice mixes.

1 pound (448 g) fingerling potatoes, cut into bite-sized pieces*
Ghee for cooking
1 red bell pepper, seeds and stem removed, flesh chopped
1 small onion, chopped
5 cloves garlic, chopped
1 tablespoon (7 g) sweet paprika (or more)
1 teaspoon caraway seeds (optional, but lends the paprikash a decidedly Hungarian flair)
Dash cayenne pepper or crushed red pepper flakes
1 tablespoon (16 ml) tomato paste
6 eggs, lightly whisked with a fork
½ cup (115 ml) plain whole-milk Greek yogurt*

Fill a large pot halfway with water and bring to a boil. Add the potatoes and simmer them for 10 minutes, or until they're tender when pierced with the tip of a sharp knife. Drain well.

While the potatoes simmer, in a large skillet, melt a generous knob of ghee over medium heat. Add the pepper and onion and cook, stirring occasionally, for 5 minutes, or until the onion is becoming translucent and fragrant. Add the garlic, paprika, caraway, cayenne and tomato paste and stir well to combine. Cook for another 5 minutes, or until the garlic is soft and fragrant.

Stir in the eggs and drained potatoes, stirring often to scramble the eggs softly, and cook for 2 minutes, or until the eggs are opaque and cooked through. Remove the skillet from the heat and stir in the yogurt. Serve immediately.

Leftover paprikash can be refrigerated for 4 days.

*To make this dish Paleo-friendly, use sweet potatoes in place of the fingerlings and Coconut Cream (see page 111) with a spritz of lemon juice in place of the yogurt.

Indian-Style Butter Chicken with Tomatoes, Chickpeas and Spinach

Makes 4 servings

India is such a diverse and wide-ranging country that it has too many classic dishes to name. It's impossible to point to the definitive Indian dish! That said, butter chicken has to be one of the top contenders. You'll use plenty of ghee in this dish so that its lush flavor infuses the chicken and veggies with a velvety savoriness and authentic flavor. Because the majority of vitamins are fat-soluble (only B and C are not), combining ghee with these vitamin-rich veggies makes them all the more nutritious. It's best to wait until the last minute to cut the basil because then it won't have time to blacken.

Ghee for cooking
1 onion, chopped
4 cloves garlic, chopped
1 pound (448 g) chicken breast, trimmed and cut into larger-than-bite-sized pieces
1 tablespoon (6 g) curry powder
Dash sea salt
1 can (15 ounces [411 g]) diced tomatoes
1 can (15 ounces or [425 g]) chickpeas, drained
10 leaves fresh basil
5 ounces (140 g) curly spinach, roughly chopped

In a large skillet, melt a large knob of ghee over medium heat. Add the onion and cook, stirring occasionally, for 5 minutes, or until the onion is translucent and fragrant. Add the garlic and reduce the heat to medium-low. Cook for 3 minutes, or until the garlic is fragrant and softened. Stir in the chicken, curry powder, salt, tomatoes and chickpeas and increase the heat to medium. Simmer for 10 to 12 minutes, or until the thickest piece of chicken is opaque when cut in half, occasionally flipping the chicken.

While the chicken cooks, stack the basil leaves into a pile and roll them into a tight tube. Cut the tube into thin slices to create ribbons. This is called a "chiffonade." When the chicken is cooked through, add the basil and spinach and cook for another minute or two, just long enough to wilt the spinach. Serve immediately.

Leftover chicken can be refrigerated for 4 days.

Coconut-Almond Cupcakes with Spiced Pumpkin Frosting

Makes 12 cupcakes

Making your own instant frosting is easy. Just stir a little maple syrup into plain whole-milk Greek yogurt, Coconut Cream, mascarpone or even ricotta cheese. All of those base ingredients are thick and rich enough to have a frosting-esque texture after you've added maple syrup. Unlike store-bought frosting made with hydrogenated oils, homemade frosting tends to lose its shape at room temperature, so keep the frosted cupcakes in the refrigerator and wait until you're nearly ready to serve them before letting them come to room temperature. Or you could make the frosting separately and keep it refrigerated, and then frost the cupcakes just before serving.

FOR THE CUPCAKES

¾ cup (68 g) almond flour
½ cup (55 g) coconut flour
¾ cup (120 g) raw buckwheat flour or brown rice flour*
1½ teaspoons (7 g) baking powder
Pinch sea salt
½ cup (120 ml) maple syrup
¼ cup (56 ml) melted ghee or butter
2 eggs
1 cup (240 ml) whole milk**
2 teaspoons (10 ml) vanilla

FOR THE FROSTING

1½ cups (345 ml) plain whole-milk Greek yogurt, the liquid whey poured off (instead of stirred back in)**
1 teaspoon vanilla
1 cup (224 g) canned pumpkin
2 tablespoons (30 ml) maple syrup or more to taste
1 teaspoon cinnamon

Preheat the oven to 375°F (190°C). Line a muffin tray with parchment paper cups.

In a large bowl, whisk together the flours, baking powder and salt.

In a smaller bowl, whisk together the maple syrup, butter, eggs, milk and vanilla. Whisk the wet ingredients into the dry ingredients and promptly pour the batter into the waiting muffin cups.

Bake for 25 to 27 minutes, or until the tops are turning golden and an inserted toothpick comes out clean.

While the cupcakes bake, stir together all of the frosting ingredients. Make sure the cupcakes are completely cooled before you frost them!

Store leftover frosted cupcakes in the refrigerator, but allow them to come to room temperature before serving them.

*These are not Paleo ingredients, but they are gluten-free and whole-grain.

**For Paleo-friendly frosting, use coconut milk instead of dairy milk and Coconut Cream (see page 111) instead of the yogurt. Note that the coconut frosting will harden substantially when refrigerated.*

> **Tip:** *Saturated fats are great to use in baked goods that need to hold their shape, such as cookies. Unsaturated fats tend to make baked goods spread as they bake. That's fine for cakes, muffins and other batters that are confined to pans and cups as they bake. But cookies, scones and other dough-based baked goods shouldn't spread.*

Brazilian Shrimp, Coconut and Cashews in Palm Oil

Makes 4 servings

Red palm oil—or dendê, as it's called in Brazil—has a rich, earthy flavor and vivid hue. The latter is because red palm oil contains more beta-carotene than any other foodstuff. Beta-carotene + fat = vitamin A, which is essential for healthy eyes, so it's not surprising that red palm oil is highly valued throughout tropical palm-growing regions. Move over, carrots! The earthy flavor of dendê is the ideal underpinning for slightly sweet bananas, tart tomatoes and creamy coconut milk. Sweet-briny shrimp top off this dish.

½ cup (43 g) unsweetened coconut flakes
1 cup (140 g) raw cashews, chopped
Red palm oil for cooking
6 cloves garlic, chopped
2 green bananas, peeled and sliced
2 large tomatoes, chopped
½ cup (120 ml) whole coconut milk
1½ pounds (672 g) wild-caught U.S. shrimp, peeled and deveined
Dash sea salt
1 small bunch cilantro, leaves only

In a large skillet, heat the coconut over medium heat. Toast for 3 minutes, shaking the skillet occasionally, or until the coconut is fragrant and turning golden brown. Transfer the toasted flakes to a cool plate.

Carefully wipe out the skillet and place the cashews in it. Return the skillet to medium heat and toast the cashews for 3 minutes, shaking the skillet occasionally, or until the cashews are fragrant and turning golden brown. Add them to the plate with the toasted coconut and wipe out the skillet again before drizzling in a generous spoonful of oil.

Place the skillet over medium-low heat. Add the garlic and bananas and cook for 3 to 5 minutes, or until the garlic is fragrant and soft. Stir in the tomatoes, milk, shrimp and salt and increase the heat to medium. Cook for 4 to 5 minutes, flipping halfway through, or until the shrimp have curled and are opaque when cut in half.

Remove the skillet from the heat and stir in the cilantro along with the toasted coconut and cashews. Or, if you prefer more of a show-stopper look, garnish each plate with those final three ingredients instead of stirring them in.

Leftover shrimp can be refrigerated for 2 days.

African-Style Cashew Chicken in Red Palm Oil

Makes 4 servings

This is an authentic African dish: Millet is one of Africa's main grains, hearty greens and chicken are favored ingredients in many parts of the continent and red palm oil is the quintessential African oil. Red palm oil has a bright red hue, and it also has a full, earthy flavor that makes it a delicious underpinning for assertive ingredients such as ginger, limes and garlic. Just be careful when handling palm oil, because once it touches fabric or anything with a porous surface, it leaves behind a bright orange stain. It's best to immediately wipe up any spills or drips with a paper towel. Also, skip wooden utensils and bowls in favor of ones made of metal, glass or black silicone.

1 cup (240 ml) water
½ cup (100 g) millet*
2 tablespoons (30 ml) red palm oil
1 yellow onion, chopped
2 pounds (896 g) chicken thighs, trimmed and cut into bite-sized pieces
6 cloves garlic, chopped
1 bunch chard, tough stems ripped away and discarded, leaves chopped
4 medium tomatoes, chopped
Juice of ½ lime
¼ cup (65 g) cashew or almond butter
1½ teaspoons (3 g) ginger
Pinch cayenne pepper
Sea salt to taste

In a medium pot, bring the water to a boil. Stir in the millet, reduce the heat to low, and simmer, covered, for 15 to 20 minutes, or until the millet has absorbed the water and has reached the desired tenderness. Fluff it with a fork and leave it uncovered.

While the millet cooks, in a large skillet, heat the oil over medium heat. Add the onion and cook for 5 minutes. Stir in the chicken, garlic and chard and cook for an additional 5 minutes, stirring occasionally to make sure the chicken is cooked evenly on all sides. Stir in the tomatoes, lime juice, cashew butter, ginger, cayenne and salt and cook for a final 4 to 5 minutes, just until the sauce has thickened. Stir the cooked millet into the chicken mixture and serve immediately.

Leftover chicken can be refrigerated for 3 days.

Millet isn't a Paleo ingredient, but it is gluten-free and whole-grain.

Tip: *Palm oil has become a controversial foodstuff in recent years. Because it's a sturdy saturated fat, it can stand in for butter. Also, because palm oil comes from a plant and not an animal, it's vegetarian-friendly. The sturdy structure of palm oil means it can take on the role that trans fats were created to play.*

But there's a caveat. When palm oil was first sourced, it was plentiful and inexpensive because it mostly comes from less-developed areas of the world. So many forests of palm trees and non-palm trees were cut down during the palm oil rush that indigenous peoples who depended on palm as an important food no longer have access to it or many other native foods.

When shopping for palm oil, look for Fair Trade brands committed to sourcing palm oil in a sustainable manner that benefits the local farmers, communities and native flora and fauna.

Hungarian-Inspired Mushroom, Beef and Tomato Soup

Makes 4 servings

Goulash is known for being hearty, flavorful and rustic. In other words, it's very Hungarian. The beefiness of the portabellas is an ideal accompaniment to, well, beef! Top sirloin is lean and easy to cut into thin strips, plus it doesn't take long to cook. Or you could use ground beef if you'd like your goulash to remind you of chili. The tomato-and-paprika base certainly does lend itself to that interpretation, especially when you consider that tomatoes and peppers originally came from the New World. (Sweet paprika is made of dried mild peppers.) But even though peppers and tomatoes aren't native to the Old World, it's hard to imagine Hungarian—or Italian or Spanish—cuisine without those ingredients.

FOR THE SOUP

Red palm oil for cooking

1 pound (448 g) cremini mushrooms, sliced (See Tip below)

1 medium onion, chopped

2 large portobello mushrooms, lightly brushed under running water (See Tip below)

½ pound (224 g) top sirloin, cut into ½" (1.2 cm-) wide strips

28 ounces (784 g) diced tomatoes

2 cups (480 ml) chicken broth

1 tablespoon (7 g) sweet paprika (or smoked/hot if you prefer)

1 tablespoon (3 g) dried thyme

4 large purple fingerling potatoes, scrubbed and cut into bite-sized cubes*
Sea salt to taste

FOR THE OPTIONAL GARNISH

1 cup (230 ml) plain whole-milk plain Greek yogurt*

½ English cucumber, minced

In a large soup pot, heat a generous spoonful of oil over medium heat. Stir in the cremini mushrooms and onion. Cook, stirring often, for 10 minutes, or until the onion is translucent and the mushrooms have shrunk to half their size.

Meanwhile, trim away the stems of the portobello mushrooms and discard them. If you like, you can scoop away the gills with a small spoon and discard those, too, or you can leave them in place if you want a darker-colored, richer mushroom flavored soup.

Cut the portobellos into thin slices and stir them into the pot. After about 10 minutes, the mushrooms should be soft and the onion fragrant. Break the portobello slices into bite-sized pieces with the edge of a spatula.

Add the sirloin and continue to cook for another 5 minutes, stirring often. Stir in the tomatoes, broth, paprika and thyme. Bring to a boil, and then reduce the heat to medium-low. Stir in the potatoes and continue to simmer for 10 minutes. Remove the pot from the heat and add salt to taste.

While the soup simmers, in a medium bowl, stir together the yogurt and cucumber (if using). Serve the hot soup garnished with the cool yogurt.

Leftover soup and yogurt can be refrigerated separately for 4 days.

For a Paleo-friendly dish, use sweet potatoes in place of the purple fingerlings and Coconut Cream (see page 111) in place of the yogurt.

> **Tips:** If a store sells mushrooms loose and pre-packaged, the loose version is often half the price of the pre-packaged version! It's okay to rinse the mushrooms because you'll be putting them in soup.

Recipes with Monounsaturated Fats: Time to Sauté, Simmer and Bake

Bacon Drippings, Schmaltz, Olive Oil, Avocado Oil, Peanut Oil, Hazelnut Oil, Almond Oil, Pistachio Oil, Macadamia Nut Oil, Pecan Oil.

Here's where you'll find the most interchangeable variety. Most nut and fruit oils (olives and avocados are fruits) fall into the monounsaturated category, and so do animal fats such as rendered poultry drippings and bacon drippings. Along with being ideal for medium- and low-heat sautéing, these oils are excellent to include in batter-based baked goods. (Unlike saturated fats, monounsaturated fats will cause baked goods to spread, so you don't want to use them in dough-based baked goods like cookies and scones.)

Avocado is the mildest-tasting oil, and it makes a great replacement for refined flavorless oils. Buttery-tasting olive oils are good choices, too. Or you might want to choose a stronger-tasting oil that complements what you're baking. How about brownies made with hazelnut oil?

Classifying monounsaturated oils as nuts, fruits or animal fats is handy when you want to swap out one oil or fat for another. For example, it's generally best to swap a nut for a nut or a fruit for a fruit because they have similar flavors. Peanut oil is the only exception in the sense that it has a very strong flavor—although heating peanut oil makes it taste considerably more mild. Of course, each oil has its own unique flavor and fragrance. That's what makes cooking with unrefined oils so much fun!

Recipe Tips: A "drizzle" of oil called for in a recipe means about 1 tablespoon (15 ml).

All herbs are dried unless listed as fresh.

Shrimp and Bacon Jambalaya with Cauliflower Rice

Makes 4 servings

Jambalaya is a classic Creole dish that's typically served atop a bed of rice. This time, though, you'll swap out the rice for cauliflower, which scores far lower on the glycemic scale because it's not a grain. The lower the score, the better. Foods high on the glycemic scale cause blood sugar levels to rise and lead to problems such as diabetes and impaired immune systems. Another perk of using cauliflower is that it cooks through in 5 minutes, whereas brown rice takes 40 minutes to cook. A win-win! It doesn't take long to run the cauliflower florets through a food processor to chop them into rice-sized pieces. If you want to go the traditional route, you could replace the cauliflower with 2 cups (330 g) of cooked brown rice. Stir it into the jambalaya when you stir in the shrimp.

½ pound (224 g) bacon
1 medium yellow onion, chopped
1 green or red bell pepper, seeds and stem removed, flesh chopped
4 ribs celery, chopped
4 green onions, trimmed and chopped
6 cloves garlic, chopped
1 cup (240 ml) vegetable broth or seafood stock
2 large tomatoes, chopped
2 bay leaves
1 tablespoon (3 g) oregano
1 tablespoon (3 g) thyme
Dash cayenne pepper
1 pound (448 g) wild-caught U.S. shrimp, peeled and deveined, each shrimp cut into 3 pieces
1 small head cauliflower, florets only, run through a food processor to cut it into small rice-sized pieces

Preheat the oven to 375°F (190°C). Line a rimmed baking sheet with aluminum foil and set a wire rack on top of the foil.

Lay the bacon strips on the wire rack, spacing them equally apart. Bake for 20 minutes, or until the bacon is sizzling and dark brown but not blackening.

Lift the rack—with the bacon still on it—out of the baking sheet and set aside. It will be hot, so protect your hands. Pour the rendered bacon drippings into a small glass jar to save it for future use. As soon as the bacon has cooled enough to comfortably handle it, coarsely chop the strips.

In a large skillet, heat a generous drizzle of the bacon drippings over medium-low heat. Stir in the onion, pepper, celery, green onions and garlic. Sauté for 5 minutes, or until the veggies are softened. Add the broth, tomatoes, bay leaves, oregano, thyme and cayenne. Bring to a boil, and then reduce the heat to low and simmer for 10 minutes.

Stir in the shrimp, cauliflower and cooked bacon and cook for 5 minutes, stirring occasionally, or until the shrimp has turned pink and opaque. Remove the mixture from the heat, remove and discard the bay leaves and serve immediately.

Leftover jambalaya can be refrigerated for 2 days. If the jambalaya looks too dry upon reheating, or at any point, add another ½ cup (120 ml) of vegetable broth or seafood stock.

Coffee-Spiked Mexican Pozole with Chicken

Makes 4 servings

Any chef worth her weight in saffron will tell you that chicken thighs are tastier than chicken breasts. Because chickens walk and run more than they flap and fly, their legs become more developed—that is, more flavorful—than their breasts. The thighs are also juicier, especially when you simmer them in soup. You may want to trim the thighs carefully to create all-meat-and-no-fat morsels, or you could allow the fat to melt into the pozole to add extra flavor. Or course, you'll also have the rich flavor of the bacon drippings to add an oomph of savoriness.

FOR THE POZOLE

Rendered schmaltz or bacon drippings for cooking (See page 135)
2 pounds (896 g) boneless skinless chicken thighs, trimmed and cut into bite-sized pieces
1 small onion, chopped
5 cloves garlic, chopped
4 cups (32 ounces [960 ml]) chicken broth
½ cup (120 ml) brewed coffee
28 ounces (784 g) diced tomatoes
1 (15 ounces [425 g]) can navy beans*
1 tablespoon (7.5 g) chili powder
Dash sea salt
1 large sweet potato, scrubbed and trimmed, flesh cut into 1" (2.5 cm) cubes
1 can (15 ounces [420 g]) yellow or white hominy**

OPTIONAL TOPPINGS

Cooked bacon, chopped
Chopped cilantro
Lime wedges
Thinly sliced cabbage
Chopped avocado
Plain whole-milk Greek yogurt*

In a large soup pot, melt a dollop of schmaltz or bacon drippings over medium heat. Add the chicken, onion and garlic and cook for 5 minutes, or until the chicken is browned. Pour in the broth and increase the heat to high. Simmer for 5 minutes.

Reduce the heat to medium and stir in the coffee, tomatoes, beans, chili powder, salt and sweet potatoes. Let the soup simmer for 10 minutes, or until the sweet potatoes have reached the desired tenderness. Stir in the hominy, simmer for another minute to heat everything through and garnish with any or all of the optional toppings.

Leftover pozole can be refrigerated for 4 days. Like all tomato-based soups and sauces, the flavor deepens upon standing.

*To make a Paleo-friendly dish, substitute green beans for the navy beans. It's best to cut them into bite-sized pieces before adding them to the soup during the final 5 minutes of cooking (i.e., when you're simmering the sweet potatoes). And instead of yogurt, use Coconut Cream (see page 111).

**Hominy is corn, which means it isn't a Paleo ingredient. But it is what makes pozole pozole.

Strawberry Pasta with Bacon, Chicken and Green Beans

Makes 4 servings

Strawberries with bacon? You bet! It's the ultimate sweet-and-savory experience. You might as well use bacon drippings for cooking, too. Look for organic strawberries. Because they're one of the top-sprayed fruits and you're going to eat the entire fruit (no peel to discard), it's worth seeking out organic berries. Fresh berries are only in season for a few short months of the year, so you can substitute frozen strawberries if you like. They'll be more watery than fresh berries, but you can add the thawed berries to the chicken during the last few minutes of cooking to evaporate some of the water and warm the berries through.

10 strips bacon (peppered if you wish)
¾ pound (336 g) chicken breasts, trimmed and cut into 1" (2.5 cm-) thick strips
4 servings whole-grain gluten-free pasta of your choice*
½ pound (224 g) green beans, trimmed and cut into bite-sized pieces
16 strawberries, hulled and sliced
Heavy cream for drizzling*

Preheat the oven to 375°F (190°C). Line a rimmed baking sheet with aluminum foil and set a wire rack on top of the foil.

Lay the bacon strips on the wire rack, spacing them equally apart. Bake for 20 minutes, or until the bacon is sizzling and dark brown but not blackening.

Lift the rack—with the bacon still on it—and pour the rendered bacon drippings into a small glass jar to save it for future use. As soon as the bacon has cooled enough to comfortably handle it, coarsely chop the strips.

In a large skillet, heat a generous drizzle of the bacon drippings over medium-low heat. Add the chicken and cook, stirring occasionally, for 5 minutes, or until the thickest strip is opaque when cut in half. Remove the pan from the heat.

Prepare the pasta according to the package directions, adding the green beans during the final 3 minutes of cooking. Drain well. Add the pasta and beans to the skillet with the chicken and stir to coat with the bacon drippings.

Add the strawberries, bacon and a drizzle of cream and stir well to combine. Serve immediately.

Leftover pasta can be refrigerated for 2 days.

*For a Paleo-friendly dish, use cooked spaghetti squash or spiraled zucchini instead of pasta and Coconut Cream (see page 111) in place of the dairy cream.

Classic Coq au Vin

Makes 4 to 6 servings

This quintessential French dish seems daunting until you actually make it. Then you realize that if you can sauté a few ingredients and put them into a roasting pan, you can make coq au vin ("chicken in wine") with the best of 'em. The hardest part is allowing everything to bake for a full hour. Your entire house will be aromatic with bacon, chicken, savory herbs and wine. Adding the mushrooms during the final 15 minutes of cooking will ensure that they don't dry out. You'll have plenty of gorgeous drippings in the pan, too, which makes an amazing gravy.

½ pound (224 g) bacon, chopped

1 large onion, chopped

3 carrots, scrubbed and chopped

4 pounds (1.7 kg) chicken parts with back, neck, wingtips and excess skin removed (Breasts, legs and thighs are all welcome in this dish; bone-in meat is what transforms this French fricassee into the heavenly meal it is!)

4 cloves garlic, chopped

1 tablespoon (3 g) thyme

2 bay leaves

1½ cups (360 ml) dry red wine

1 pound (448 g) cremini or button mushrooms, sliced

Preheat the oven to 350°F (180°C) and have a large roasting pan ready.

In a large skillet, cook the bacon, onion and carrots over medium heat for 10 minutes, or until the bacon is starting to crisp and the onion and carrots are browning. Add the chicken and garlic and continue to cook for 10 minutes, or until the chicken is browned.

Transfer everything to a roasting pan, being sure to get every last drip out of that skillet into the pan. Sprinkle on the thyme and bay leaves and pour the wine over everything. Cover and bake for 45 minutes. Gently stir the mushrooms into the chicken and bake for another 15 minutes—for a total baking time of 1 hour. Cut into a thick piece of chicken to make sure the juices run clear, or use a meat thermometer to make sure chicken is done before serving it. The internal temperature should be 180°F (82°C). Remove and discard the bay leaves before serving.

Leftovers can be refrigerated for 5 days or frozen for 3 months.

Tip: This utterly divine dish is lovely on its own or served with skin-on mashed potatoes or sweet potatoes.

Mushroom, Chorizo and Lentil Stir-Fry

Makes 4 servings

Chorizo may be fresh uncooked sausage sold in casings, or it may have already been cured. If it's cured, simply cut it into slices, remove the outer skin and chop the chorizo to create small pieces. If it's fresh chorizo, squeeze the chorizo out of its natural casing when you add it to the skillet, and then use the edge of a spatula or spoon to break up the chorizo as it cooks. Cured chorizo won't be as tender as fresh chorizo, but it has a deeper, more intense flavor, plus cured chorizo can be kept in the refrigerator for at least a month—and it makes a great last-minute snack!

2 cups (480 ml) water
1 cup (192 g) brown lentils*
Schmaltz for cooking (See page 135)
2 pounds (896 g) cremini or button mushrooms, sliced
2 large onions, chopped
1 pound (448 g) chorizo
1 bunch chard, ends trimmed, leaves chopped

In a medium pot, bring the water to a boil. Stir in the lentils, reduce the heat to medium-low and simmer for 20 to 25 minutes, or until the lentils have reached the desired tenderness. Drain well.

While the lentils simmer, in a large skillet, melt a dab of schmaltz over medium heat. Add the mushrooms and onions and cook, stirring occasionally, for 8 to 10 minutes, or until the mushrooms have shrunk to half their size. Stir in the chorizo and cook for 3 to 5 minutes, or until the chorizo has cooked through. Stir in the chard and cook 2 to 4 minutes, or just until the chard has begun to wilt. Stir in the drained lentils and remove the skillet from the heat promptly. Serve immediately.

Leftover stir-fry can be refrigerated for 3 days.

Lentils are not a Paleo ingredient, but they are a whole, unprocessed food.

> **Tips:** *You can use rendered duck or goose fat in place of schmaltz. Roast a duck or goose to render it as you would render schmaltz. Bear in mind that ducks and geese have more insulating fat and can be messier to roast than a chicken. Or look for rendered duck or goose fat at farmers' markets or in stores offering pastured animal products.*
>
> *Chorizo is normally fairly spicy, so this recipe doesn't call for additional spices or salt, but feel free to sprinkle your stir-fry with sea salt and/or chili powder if you like.*

Old-Fashioned Potato Salad with Roasted Chicken and Schmaltz

Makes 4 servings

Forget potato salad made with store-bought mayo! It's much better to make your own with plain whole-milk Greek yogurt or Coconut Cream. (See page 111.) For Old World flair, you'll add tangy vinegar and aromatic dill along with the velvety hard-boiled eggs and crunchy cucumber. This potato salad is extra-savory thanks to the schmaltz. Even if you don't wind up with a piece of roasted chicken in every bite, its flavor will still be there. (Tip: If you don't use all of a roasted chicken when you make it, freeze it to use later. Just let the meat thaw for about a day in the refrigerator before enjoying it.) If you'd like a confetti effect for your potato salad, look for purple, red and golden fingerling potatoes. This is the perfect dish to serve on the 4th of July or at a Memorial Day barbecue!

FOR THE DRESSING

¼ cup + 2 tablespoons (90 ml) schmaltz (See page 135)

¼ cup (58 ml) plain whole-milk Greek yogurt*

2 tablespoons (30 ml) red wine vinegar

1 tablespoon (3 g) dill

¾ teaspoon sea salt

FOR THE SALAD

1 pound (448 g) fingerling potatoes, scrubbed and cut into bite-sized pieces*

4 eggs

1 pound (448 g) roasted chicken, chopped (See page 186)

2 green onions, green parts only, minced

1 small cucumber, unpeeled but seeds removed, chopped, or 3 ribs celery, trimmed and chopped

In a screw top jar, place all of the dressing ingredients and close the lid firmly. Shake well.

Fill a medium pot halfway with water and bring to a boil. Add the potatoes and reduce the heat to medium. Simmer, covered, for 10 minutes. Drain well.

Place the eggs in the dry pot and add enough water to cover. Bring to a boil, and then reduce the heat to medium-low and simmer, half-covered, for 10 minutes. Remove the pot from the heat and run cold water into the pot to quickly lower the temperature. This will prevent the eggs from overcooking. Let the eggs sit in the cold water until they're cool enough to handle.

Peel the eggs, and then coarsely chop them. Place the eggs in a large mixing bowl and add the cooked potatoes, chicken, onions and cucumber. Toss well. Pour on the dressing and toss well to coat. Serve immediately.

Leftover salad can be refrigerated for 2 days.

For a Paleo-friendly dish, use Coconut Cream (see page 111) in place of the yogurt and sweet potatoes in place of the fingerlings.

Walnut-Raspberry Muffins

Makes 18 muffins

Berries are tender fruits, which means that muffins made with berries have a hauntingly fresh appeal. You could replace the raspberries in these muffins with blueberries, blackberries or even sliced strawberries. Or mulberries if it's June and you're lucky enough to have a mulberry tree in the neighborhood. Pretty much any berry pairs well with nuts and spices. Enjoy these muffins for breakfast or as a dessert. To make the latter, top the muffins with some homemade whipped cream and a drizzle of maple syrup. Stash your berry muffins in the fridge to prevent the berries from fermenting or turning moldy. Or you can freeze them and enjoy them later.

1 cup (90 g) almond flour
1 cup (120 g) buckwheat flour*
¼ cup (40 g) brown rice or teff or sorghum flour*
½ cup (80 g) sucanat or palm sugar
2 teaspoons (9 g) baking powder
½ teaspoon baking soda
Dash salt
1 tablespoon (7 g) cinnamon
1½ teaspoons (3 g) nutmeg
1 cup (100 g) chopped walnuts
¼ cup (60 ml) extra-virgin olive oil
3 eggs
7 ounces (196 ml) whole-milk plain Greek yogurt**
¼ cup (60 ml) whole milk**
1 teaspoon vanilla
6 ounces (168 g) fresh raspberries, rinsed and drained well

Preheat the oven to 375°F (190°C). Line 2 muffin tins with 18 parchment-paper muffin cups.

In a large bowl, whisk together the flours, sucanat, baking powder, baking soda, salt, cinnamon, nutmeg and walnuts.

In another bowl, whisk together the oil, eggs, yogurt, milk and vanilla. Stir in the raspberries. Stir the wet ingredients into the dry ones until the batter is well blended.

Scoop the batter into the muffin cups, filling each one about ¾ full, and bake for 25 minutes, or until a toothpick inserted into the center-most muffin comes out clean and warm and the tops are turning golden brown.

Leftover muffins can be refrigerated for 4 days or frozen for 1 month.

These flours are not Paleo ingredients, but they are gluten-free and whole-grain.

**To make this dish more Paleo-friendly, use Coconut Cream (see page 111) in place of the yogurt and coconut milk in place of the whole milk.*

Pan-Fried Beet Chips with Artichoke Tapenade

Makes about 1½ cups (475 g) tapenade

Traditionally, tapenade is made with olives, but in this version, the main ingredient is artichoke hearts. The salty aspect of brined artichokes means they make a better tapenade than frozen or fresh artichokes, plus they're easier to use. Just whirl them through a food processor with the remaining ingredients, and you've got tapenade! The creamy whole-milk Greek yogurt provides a lush background to the brined artichoke and salty capers, but if you'd rather have a more traditional non-creamy tapenade, simply omit the yogurt. Either version is tasty with the beet chips. Because extra-virgin olive oil is in both the tapenade and the chips, you'll still enjoy a hint of olive flavor.

FOR THE TAPENADE

Extra-virgin olive oil for cooking

2 cloves garlic, chopped

14 ounces (400 g) brined artichoke hearts, drained

2 teaspoons (6 g) capers, drained

Juice of ¼ lemon

1 teaspoon thyme

¼ cup (58 ml) plain whole-milk Greek yogurt*

FOR THE CHIPS

Extra-virgin olive oil for cooking

2 raw beets, peeled and cut into thin slices

Sea salt for sprinkling

In a small skillet, sauté the oil and garlic over medium-low heat for 3 minutes, or until the garlic is fragrant and starting to turn golden brown. Transfer the mixture to a food processor and add the remaining tapenade ingredients. Blend until smooth.

In a large skillet, heat the oil over medium heat. Add the beets, arranging them in a single layer so that none overlap. You'll need to cook them in batches. Cook them for 8 to 10 minutes, or until both sides are turning golden brown, flipping the beets halfway through.

Remove the beets to a plate covered with paper towels and sprinkle them with salt. With each batch of beets, you might have to cook them for less time because the pan will be hotter (or reduce the heat slightly). Serve the chips with the tapenade.

The chips are best eaten promptly, but leftover tapenade can be refrigerated for 4 days.

*Omit the yogurt for a Paleo-friendly tapenade.

Sausage, Red Bean and Spinach Stew with Homemade Hot Pepper Oil

Makes 4 servings

Infusing oil is as simple as choosing your flavors—spices, herbs, citrus zests, etc.—and then gently heating them with an oil and giving the flavors time to blend. Oils that are primarily monounsaturated are your best bet. They can handle a little direct heat, and they won't solidify when they cool, which makes them easy to drizzle onto dishes as an elegant finishing touch. You can store your infused oil in the refrigerator for a week in a tightly closed glass jar or bottle. Because dried spices are more shelf-stable than fresh herbs or citrus zest, oils infused with dried spices can be refrigerated for 2 weeks. Try adding this hot pepper oil to soups, salads, omelets or anything else you'd like to spice up.

FOR THE HOT PEPPER OIL
½ cup (120 ml) extra-virgin olive oil
1 teaspoon crushed red pepper flakes

FOR THE STEW
Extra-virgin olive oil for cooking
1 large yellow onion, chopped
6 cloves garlic, chopped
1 pound (448 g) pork sausage links, outer casings removed (such as fresh chorizo)
15 ounces (425 g) red beans, undrained*
28 ounces (784 g) diced tomatoes
4 cups (32 ounces [960 ml]) chicken broth
2 tablespoons (5.4 g) thyme
2 tablespoons (6 g) oregano
8 ounces (224 g) curly spinach or kale, roughly chopped (If using kale, remove the tough stems.)
Sea salt to taste

In a small pot, combine the oil and pepper, and then allow to stand over low heat for 5 minutes. Remove the pot from the heat and let the oil stand and infuse while you make the stew.

In a large soup pot, heat a generous drizzle of the oil over medium heat. Stir in the onion and cook for 4 minutes, or until the onion is softened. Add the garlic and sausage, stirring to break up the sausage, and cook another 3 minutes, or just until the sausage is starting to brown. Stir in the beans, tomatoes, broth, thyme and oregano. Bring them to a brief boil, and then reduce the heat to medium-low and simmer for 15 minutes. Stir in the spinach and continue to simmer for another 5 minutes, or until the spinach is soft. Season with salt to taste. Serve the stew immediately, drizzling each portion with the hot pepper oil. If you like, you can pour the oil into a small decanter and allow your diners to do their own drizzling.

Let the oil cool completely to room temperature before transferring it to a screw-top jar with a tightly closing lid. You can refrigerate the oil for 2 weeks. Just be sure to let it come to room temperature before using it so that it'll pour easily.

Leftover stew can be refrigerated for 4 days or frozen for 2 months. Anything with a tomato sauce base freezes beautifully. If it's too thick upon reheating, stir in more broth to thin the stew.

For a Paleo-friendly dish, substitute ¾ pound (336 g) freshly cooked green beans for the canned red beans. Stir them in during the final 5 minutes of simmering.

> ***Tip:*** *Extra-virgin olive oil makes a nice conditioner for frizzy or dry hair. Rub a teaspoonful into your hands and run them through your hair, whether you've just gotten out of the shower or you're dealing with dry-winter frizz. No need to rinse it out!*

Chili-Lime Garlic Shrimp with Homemade Guacamole

Makes 4 servings

Guacamole is magnificent as a dip, a spread or paired with dishes such as this spicy, garlicky shrimp. Some people insist on adding cumin to their guacamole, while others detest it. Some people like to add chipotle or minced jalapeños, while other people don't want much heat. This recipe falls more into the classic "unadorned guacamole" category, but feel free to tweak the ingredients to give the guacamole a cumin- or pepper-laced flair. If you do want to try adding cumin, stir ½ teaspoon into the guacamole, taste it and then add more spice until you've hit your cumin comfort level. The lemon or lime juice, too, should be added to taste.

FOR THE GUACAMOLE

1 ripe avocado, flesh only
2 medium tomatoes, chopped
2 green onions, green parts only, minced
1 small clove garlic, minced
1 small bunch cilantro, leaves only, chopped
Squeeze of lemon or lime juice
Sea salt for sprinkling

FOR THE SHRIMP

Avocado oil for cooking
1½ pounds (672 g) wild-caught U.S. shrimp, peeled and deveined
8 cloves garlic, chopped
1 tablespoon (8 g) chili powder
Freshly squeezed lime juice

OPTIONAL GARNISHES

Cooked brown rice*
Toasted 100 percent corn tortillas*
Whole-milk plain Greek yogurt*
Chopped lettuce
Lime wedges

Place the avocado in a small bowl. Use a fork to smash the avocado into a smooth paste. Stir in the tomatoes, onions, garlic, cilantro and lemon or lime juice, starting out with just a suggestion of each and tasting to see if you would like to add more. If you want a brighter flavor, add more citrus juice. Season with salt to taste. Cover the guacamole with plastic wrap, pressing the wrap onto the surface of the guacamole to prevent air from getting to it, and refrigerate until you're ready to serve the shrimp.

In a large skillet, heat a generous drizzle of oil over medium heat. Add the shrimp, garlic and chili powder and cook, shaking the pan occasionally, for 3 to 4 minutes, flipping the shrimp halfway through. The shrimp will curl and contract as it cooks. Test the shrimps' doneness by cutting the biggest one in half to see if it's opaque all the way through.

Transfer the shrimp to a plate. Drizzle the skillet with the lime juice, and then gently scrape the bits free from the bottom of the skillet and trickle them over each serving of shrimp. Include a generous spoonful of guacamole with each serving. Serve the shrimp as is or with the suggested garnishes.

Leftover shrimp can be refrigerated for 2 days. If the guacamole is well covered with plastic wrap, it can be refrigerated for 3 days.

These are not Paleo-friendly ingredients.

Coffee, Coconut and Cocoa Granola

Makes about 6 cups (500 g) granola

Granola is surprisingly easy to make. It's a simple matter of choosing your ingredients, tossing them with a hint of fruity oil such as avocado or olive along with a drizzle of maple syrup or honey, and then popping everything into the oven. Because you want your granola to be crunchy, you may have to bake it for longer than 10 minutes, depending on your ingredients. This recipe calls for already-cooked ingredients such as toasted nuts and puffed grains, so this batch won't take long. Plus you don't want to scorch the cocoa powder and coffee. Once your granola has cooled, store it in a glass container, and then enjoy it as breakfast or as a take-along snack. Coconut milk is a natural pair for this coconut-containing granola.

3 cups (63 g) puffed millet*
2 cups (160 g) gluten-free rolled oats*
¼ cup (16 g) unsweetened cocoa powder, preferably non–Dutched
¼ cup (12 g) freshly ground coffee (Finely ground is best)
Pinch sea salt
½ cup (43 g) unsweetened flaked coconut
¼ cup (36 g) hemp seeds, chia seeds, chopped sunflower seeds or a mixture
¼ cup (60 ml) avocado oil
¼ cup (60 ml) maple syrup
½ cup (68 g) chopped roasted macadamia nuts, chopped toasted pecans, chopped toasted walnuts or a mixture

Preheat the oven to 350°F (180°C) and line 2 rimmed baking sheets with parchment paper.

In a large bowl, stir together all of the ingredients except the macadamia nuts. Which, by the way, should be stored in the fridge to prevent them from becoming rancid.

Spread the granola out on the prepared baking sheets. Bake for 10 minutes, and then pour the mixture back into the large bowl and stir in the macadamia nuts. Transfer the mixture to a large plate and let it cool.

Completely cooled granola can be stored in glass jars and kept at room temperature for 5 days.

Because grains are not Paleo-friendly, if you'd like a Paleo version of granola, use a mixture of coarsely chopped nuts in place of the grains and also include more seeds.

Wild Salmon Cakes with Sun-Dried Tomatoes

Makes about 8 cakes, or enough for 4 light servings (Feel free to double the recipe.)

Once the glorious tomato-rich days of summer have passed, one of the best ways to enjoy the full flavor of tomatoes is to include sun-dried tomatoes in your recipes. Like any dried fruit, sun-dried tomatoes have a leathery texture, but a 30-minute soak in hot water is all they need to soften. In this recipe, you'll add them to the salmon cakes for a boost of summery, sweet-tart flavor, so it's best to give the tomatoes a chance to soak and become tender. Be sure to buy tomatoes that are simply dried and bagged, not packed in oil, which is inevitably not a good-quality oil.

1 ounce (28 g) sun-dried tomatoes, cut into strips (You can often find them pre-julienned.)

Avocado oil for cooking

1 small onion, minced

4 cloves garlic, minced

7½ ounces (210 g) wild canned salmon, drained, or leftover cooked salmon

2 teaspoons (2 g) dill, plus more for garnishing

1 egg

2 tablespoons (30 ml) plain whole-milk Greek yogurt, plus more for garnishing*

¾ cup (68 g) almond flour

In a small bowl, place the tomatoes and cover them with boiling water. Let the tomatoes soak for 30 minutes, and then drain.

In a large skillet, heat a generous drizzle of oil over medium-low heat. Add the onion and cook for 3 minutes, or until the onion starts to soften. Stir in the garlic and cook an additional 3 minutes, or until the garlic is just beginning to turn golden brown around the edges.

Transfer the garlic and onion to a large bowl. Add the remaining ingredients to the sautéed onion and garlic and stir well. With a ¼-cup (60-ml) measuring cup, measure the mixture into patties, tapping each one out of the cup into your hand and shaping them into rough patties. Place them on a large plate as you go.

Add more oil to the skillet and warm it over medium heat. Place 4 of the patties into the skillet, using your hands to form each patty into smoother, rounder patties one by one as you add them to the skillet. Use a spatula to gently press down on the patties to slightly flatten them. Cook the patties for 3 minutes, and then carefully flip them over. Cook the patties for another 2 to 3 minutes, or until both sides are golden brown. Add more oil to the skillet and repeat with the remaining patties. Serve the warm patties with a dollop of yogurt and a sprinkling of dill for garnish.

Leftover salmon cakes can be refrigerated for 5 days. These make a lovely next-day breakfast when served with a poached egg on top!

For a Paleo-friendly dish, use Coconut Cream (see page 111) in place of the Greek yogurt.

Tip: *Monounsaturated oils last longer when they are refrigerated. They'll get a little cloudy and semi-liquid when chilled, but if you need to make them fully liquid, set the bottles of oil in a bowl filled with warm water. Or store them at room temperature if you'll use them within six months.*

Deep-Fried Lotus Chips

Makes appetizers for 2

Lotus flowers are more than just pretty. Underneath the blooms lie thick roots that can be thinly sliced and fried to make lacy chips. "Lacy" may sound like a strange way to describe a chip, but once you've sliced a lotus root, you'll see that it has more holes than Swiss cheese. Those holes make lotus roots the ideal candidate for frying because the oil can penetrate more evenly into each slice. Any oil suitable for medium or high heat pairs well with lotus root, which tastes vaguely nutty and sweet. Peanut oil is a particularly good match. It enhances the slight nuttiness of the lotus roots and lends them a pretty golden hue, making their lacy look even more appealing.

Lotus root
Peanut oil for frying
Sea salt for sprinkling

To prepare your lotus chips, slice off the ends of the lotus root and discard them. Using a vegetable peeler, peel away the skin and cut the root into thin slices. If you're not overly speedy in the kitchen, drop the slices in a bowl of cold water to keep them from turning brown. Be sure to pat them dry before frying them.

In a shallow, small skillet, heat the oil over medium heat, adding just enough oil to cover the bottom of the pan.

Slip in as many chips as the pan will allow—you don't want them to overlap—and cook them undisturbed for 3 minutes, or until the edges are golden brown. Use tongs or a slotted spatula to flip each chip. Continue cooking for another 2 minutes, or until both sides are brown. Repeat with the remaining chips, adding more oil if necessary and/or reducing the heat to medium-low if the oil is sputtering.

Place the cooked chips on paper towels to drain and sprinkle them with a dash of salt. Serve immediately.

If you have leftover chips, which is doubtful, you can leave the chips folded up in paper towels and clipped shut. Leave the chips on the counter and enjoy them the next day.

Bacon, Blueberry and Brussels Sprouts with Baby Spinach and Blue Cheese

Makes 4 servings

If you've been looking for a better way to make bacon, here's the answer: Bake it. The best way to get perfectly crisp bacon and have no mess to clean up afterward is to lay the strips on wire racks that are perched atop a foil-covered rimmed baking sheet/jelly roll pan. That way, once the bacon is done, you can pour the rendered bacon drippings into a jar for later use, and then discard the foil lining. Voilà! You have a clean baking sheet. Aluminum foil is less messy because it's easier to press firmly into the corners of baking sheets, but if you prefer, you can use parchment paper. Be sure to use a rimmed baking sheet to prevent the grease from dripping out and splattering onto the oven floor. Besides, you don't want to waste those lovely drippings!

1 pound (448 g) Brussels sprouts (about 24 sprouts), outermost leaves stripped away and discarded, sprouts cut in half
Peanut oil for roasting
1 pound (448 g) bacon
5 ounces (140 g) baby spinach
¼ cup (60 ml) extra-virgin olive oil
2 tablespoons (30 ml) apple cider vinegar
6 ounces (168 g) fresh blueberries, rinsed and drained
4 ounces (112 g) blue cheese*

Arrange the oven racks so that they're spaced in the upper and lower third of the oven, and then preheat the oven to 375°F (190°C). Cover a baking sheet with parchment paper. Cover a second, rimmed baking sheet with aluminum foil. Set a wire rack on top.

Toss the Brussels sprouts in a medium bowl with a drizzle of the peanut oil and then arrange them on the parchment-covered baking sheet.

Lay the bacon strips out over the wire rack, spacing them equally apart.

Place the sprouts on the bottom rack and the bacon on the top rack of the oven. Bake for 20 minutes, or until the bacon is sizzling and dark brown but not blackening and the sprouts are golden brown. Or use precooked bacon and only roast the sprouts. If the bacon is already cooked, chop it and then warm it in a skillet over medium heat for a few minutes, or until it's crisp and sizzling.

Lift the rack—with the bacon still on it—out of the baking sheet and set aside. It will be hot, so protect your hands. Pour the rendered bacon drippings into a small glass jar to save it for future use. As soon as the bacon has cooled enough to comfortably handle it, coarsely chop the strips and place them in a large bowl. Add the remaining ingredients and toss well. Serve immediately.

*If you'd like a Paleo-friendly meal, omit the cheese.

Roasted Green Beans with Sautéed Salami, Green Onions and Pine Nuts

Makes 4 servings

Most people think of salami as lunchmeat, but it can be so much more. You can dice it the way you would dice ham and include it in everything from macaroni and cheese to soups and salads. Or, as in this recipe, you can sauté salami as part of a stir-fry. Just be sure to purchase the salami as one large piece so that you can chop it into cubes. Sautéing the salami with the veggies will infuse the entire dish with the spicy savoriness of the salami; no other seasoning is needed. Any kind of salami works. Roasting the green beans rather than simmering them makes them extra-savory, too, and topping the entire dish with juicy, tart-sweet tomatoes adds another level of savory appeal. Bon appétit!

1½ pounds (672 g) green beans, rinsed, trimmed, and cut into bite-sized lengths

Peanut oil for roasting

Sea salt for sprinkling

1 pound (448 g) salami, outer skin removed, cut into ½" (1.2 cm) cubes

1 bunch green onions, trimmed and minced

½ cup (68 g) pine nuts, raw or toasted

1 pint (336 g) cherry or grape tomatoes, cut in half

Preheat the oven to 375°F (190°C) and cover 2 baking sheets with parchment paper.

In a bowl, toss the beans with a drizzle of the oil and a sprinkling of salt. (You want enough oil to lightly coat the beans, but there's no need to drown them.) Spread the beans out on the prepared baking sheets in a single layer and roast for 15 minutes, or until the beans are just starting to turn golden brown. Transfer the beans to a large bowl.

In a skillet, heat the salami over medium-low heat. As soon as it starts to cook, add the onions and pine nuts. Cook for 3 to 5 minutes, or until the onions have softened and the salami is turning ever-so-slightly golden brown.

Transfer the salami mixture to the bowl with the beans and stir in the tomatoes. Serve promptly.

Leftovers can be refrigerated for 4 days.

Pan-Fried Rainbow Trout with Wilted Spinach, Leeks and Hazelnut Oil

Makes 4 servings

Prepping leeks may sound complicated, but once you've cleaned one or two, you'll feel like a pro. Dirt stubbornly clings to leeks, so don't be shy about rubbing the layers under running water to get them scrupulously clean. The nice thing about leeks is that once you've cleaned them, you can freeze the prepped leeks for future use. Or if you have some extra cooked leeks on hand, stash them in the fridge and use them in omelets, soups and salads. Leeks are a versatile ingredient that's much appreciated in other countries—Dutch cooks adore them—but are underappreciated in the United States. It's time to remedy that!

4 leeks
Hazelnut oil for cooking
3 cloves garlic, thinly sliced
10 ounces (280 g) curly spinach
Dash sea salt
1½ pounds (672 g) rainbow trout, rinsed and patted dry

To prepare the leeks, peel off the outermost layer of each leek and discard it. Cut away the tough ends of the outer green layers, trimming each one individually. (You'll know you've gotten to the more tender part of the leek when you see light green layers.) Poke a very sharp knife through the center of the leek about 1" (2.5 cm) away from the intact bottom. Pull the knife through the layers, heading to the green ends and going all the way through. Flip the leek a quarter-turn and repeat. In effect, you're quartering the leek while keeping its end intact. You should now be able to fan out the layers. Rinse the leek thoroughly under cold running water, rubbing the layers with your fingers to dislodge the dirt. Whack the leek against the edge of the sink to dry it, and then chop it, discarding the white bottoms.

In a large skillet, heat the oil over medium heat and add the leeks. Cook, stirring occasionally, for 10 minutes. Reduce the heat to medium-low and continue to cook for another 10 minutes. Stir in the garlic and cook for 10 minutes, again stirring occasionally. Gradually stir in the spinach, turning it over often to wilt the leaves. It should be nicely wilted within 10 minutes. Season the spinach with salt. Remove the skillet from the heat, covering it to keep warm.

In another large skillet, heat another drizzle of oil over medium-low heat and add the trout, placing the filet(s) skin-side-up and working in batches if necessary. Cover and cook the trout for 5 minutes, and then gently flip it and continue cooking for another 3 minutes, still covered, or until the trout flakes apart easily and is opaque all the way through. Serve the trout with a side of the spinach and leeks.

Leftover trout can be refrigerated for 2 days; leftover spinach can be refrigerated for 4 days.

Herbed Brussels Sprouts Sautéed with Chicken, Water Chestnuts and Pomegranate Seeds

Makes 4 servings

When shopping for pomegranates, you can either buy the seeds or the whole fruit. The latter is less expensive, of course, and you can refrigerate the leftover seeds for a week. They make a great snack or last-minute garnish. To de-seed a pomegranate, cut it into quarters on a nonporous cutting board (the juice will stain the wood!), and then submerge each quarter one at a time in a large bowl of cool water. Pull the seeds free with your fingertips, letting the cream-colored mesh surrounding the seeds float up as the heavy seeds sink. Scoop away and discard the floating mesh before draining the seeds in a colander. The sweet-tart seeds are a perfect partner for the nutty hazelnut oil and earthy Brussels sprouts.

Hazelnut oil for cooking
1 pound (448 g) Brussels sprouts, outermost layers stripped away and sprouts cut in half
1 pound (448 g) chicken breast, trimmed and cut into 1" (2.5 cm-) thick strips
1 tablespoon (2 g) basil
1 tablespoon (3 g) thyme
½ teaspoon sea salt
8 ounces (224 g) sliced water chestnuts, drained
Seeds from ½ pomegranate (3 to 4 ounces [84 g to 112 g])

Drizzle enough oil into a large skillet to barely cover the bottom, and then place the sprouts flat-side-down on the skillet, arranging them so that each half is touching the surface of the skillet. Cover the skillet and let the sprouts cook undisturbed over medium-low heat for 7 minutes.

Shake the skillet to make sure the sprouts aren't sticking, and then add the chicken, basil, thyme and salt. Continue to sauté for another 5 minutes, or until the thickest piece of chicken is opaque when cut in half.

Stir in the water chestnuts and pomegranate seeds and heat through for another minute. Serve immediately, drizzling with additional hazelnut oil if you'd like a pronounced nutty flavor.

Leftover sauté can be refrigerated for 4 days. If you like, you can chop the leftover chicken, sprouts and chestnuts to repurpose the leftovers as a chilled chopped salad.

Hazelnut Mesquite Brownies

Makes an 8"x 8"(20 cm x 20 cm) pan of brownies

Anyone with a barbecue in the backyard has probably used mesquite chips to impart a lovely smoky flavor to whatever is on the grill. Those chips come from the wood of chopped-down mesquite trees. Bet you didn't know that the same tree bears edible pods that can be ground up into flour! After all, "flour" can be made from anything that's dry enough to pulverize. Mesquite flour is reminiscent of mesquite wood. It also lends a smoky, caramelized flavor to dishes. Because mesquite flour is incorporated directly into batters and rubs, its flavor is much more pronounced than the chips. It's best to use mesquite as only 25 percent of the total blend of flours for any given recipe. That way, you'll have a pleasant caramel undertone that pairs especially well with chocolate, coffee and nuts.

⅓ **cup (88 ml) hazelnut oil, plus more for greasing the pan**
3½ ounces (100 g) 85 percent dark chocolate
4 eggs
½ cup (120 ml) maple syrup
1 teaspoon coffee or vanilla extract
1 cup (90 g) almond or hazelnut flour
¼ cup (30 g) mesquite flour
¼ cup (16 g) cocoa powder, preferably non–Dutched
2 teaspoons (9 g) baking powder
Dash sea salt

Preheat the oven to 350°F (180°C) and thoroughly grease an 8"× 8" (20 cm x 20 cm) pan with a drizzle of the oil.

Break the chocolate into chunks and place them in a small pot. Heat the chocolate on the lowest setting to allow it to slowly melt. Stir often and remove the pan from the heat while there are still a few bumps in the chocolate and then finish melting it by gently swirling the pan.

In a large mixing bowl, beat the eggs for at least 1 minute. You want them to be soft and foamy. Add the maple syrup, vanilla, ⅓ cup (88 ml) of the oil and the melted chocolate and beat again. Stir in the flours, cocoa powder, baking powder and salt.

Scoop the batter into the greased pan and bake for 35 minutes, or until a toothpick inserted into the center comes out clean.

Tip: Extremely well-stocked bulk stores (like Rainbow in San Francisco) sometimes have mesquite flour, but I typically order mine from The Mesquitery or another online source.

Roasted Peppers, Olives, Lamb and Mixed Greens

Makes 4 servings

Great olives are like great olive oils. They have unique flavors, yet they all taste fresh and bright. Some olives are distinctly buttery; others are peppery. Arbequina, for example, falls into the latter category, while Castelvetrano is so mild and rich-tasting that even people who think they don't like olives find themselves reaching for another one of the fat, round, light-green olives. As a general rule, green olives are milder-tasting and firmer-textured than black olives, and brine-cured olives are saltier and firmer than oil-cured olives. Just be sure to choose pitted olives if you'll be chopping them or tossing them in with other ingredients. You don't want to accidentally bite down on a pit.

2 bell peppers, whichever color you prefer (Green is the least sweet; red is the sweetest.)
½ pound (224 g) pitted olives (Great choices include Castelvetrano, green Niçoise and Arbequina.)
Extra-virgin olive oil for roasting
Almond oil for cooking and drizzling
1 pound (448 g) ground lamb
4 cloves garlic, chopped
1 tablespoon (3 g) rosemary
Mixed greens of your choice
Sea salt to taste

First, roast the peppers: Place a piece of foil in a rimmed baking sheet and position it in the center of the middle oven rack, and then place the whole peppers directly on the oven rack over the sheet. The sheet will catch the drips; otherwise, you'll have a messy oven to clean. Roast for at least 20 minutes at 450°F (230°C). When the skin is blistered and blackening, remove the peppers and let them sit until they're cool enough to handle, and then peel away the skin and discard the stem and seeds. Cut the roasted peppers into thin strips.

While the peppers cool, reduce the oven temperature to 325°F (170°C). Place the olives in a small oven-proof ceramic or glass dish and drizzle them with a small splash of extra-virgin olive oil. Roll the olives around in the dish to coat them, and then roast them for 20 minutes, or until they're starting to shrivel and shrink. When the olives are cool enough to handle, coarsely chop.

While the olives roast, in a large skillet, heat a drizzle of the almond oil over medium heat for 1 minute before adding the lamb and garlic. Cook, stirring often to break up the lamb, for a minute or two before adding the rosemary. Continue to cook for another 3 minutes, or until the lamb has cooked through.

Remove the skillet from the heat and stir in the roasted peppers and olives, and then transfer the mixture to a large bowl and toss with the greens and a generous drizzling of almond oil. Season with salt to taste. Serve immediately.

If you think you'll have leftovers, don't toss the greens with the other ingredients. Sans greens, the dish can be refrigerated for 4 days. You can top the greens with the lamb mixture instead.

Sweet-and-Sour Lamb with Eggplant, Sweet Potato and Cauliflower

Makes 4 servings

Many dishes from the Middle East rely on a careful blend of sweet and sour. After all, in that region of the world, sweet date palms grow alongside groves of limes and lemons. When you're shopping for the ingredients in this recipe, look for pomegranate molasses in the Middle Eastern section of mainstream grocers or visit ethnic markets that cater to Middle Eastern shoppers. (Pomegranate molasses is essentially pomegranate juice that has been boiled down to a thick molasses-like consistency.) Thanks to its inherent sweet/tart balance, pomegranate molasses works well in any dish that calls for a sweet-and-sour flavor base, so you might want to try it in Asian dishes, too, where sauces are often crafted to strike that delicate balance.

1 large sweet potato, scrubbed and cut into 1" (2.5 cm) cubes

1 small head cauliflower, cut into individual bite-sized florets

Extra-virgin olive oil for cooking

1 large eggplant, skin on but ends trimmed, cut into ½" (1.2 cm-) thick slices

6 green onions, trimmed and sliced

4 cloves garlic, minced

½ teaspoon sea salt (or more to taste)

2 tablespoons (14 g) cumin

2 tablespoons (36 ml) pomegranate molasses

2 tablespoons (30 ml) balsamic vinegar

1 tablespoon (15 ml) maple syrup

Juice of ½ lemon

1 pound (448 g) ground lamb

A generous drizzle of almond oil, for garnishing

Fill a large pot halfway with water and bring to a boil over high heat. Add the sweet potatoes and reduce the heat to medium. Simmer for 5 minutes, and then add the cauliflower and simmer for an additional 5 minutes. Drain well.

In large skillet, heat a drizzle of olive oil with the eggplant over medium heat. As soon as the eggplant starts to sizzle, carefully pour in about 1 tablespoon (15 ml) water and cover the skillet. Reduce the heat to medium-low and cook undisturbed for 10 minutes. Stir in the onions and garlic and cook for 5 minutes.

Add the remaining ingredients and cook for 3 to 5 minutes, or until the lamb is cooked through, stirring often to break up the lamb. Remove the skillet from the heat and stir in the drained potatoes and cauliflower. Drizzle with a splash of almond oil before serving.

Leftovers can be refrigerated for 4 days.

> ***Tip:*** *Making a marinade? Monounsaturated oils are liquid at room temperature, so they're easy to drizzle and toss with whatever you're marinating, plus they can handle medium heat, so they're suitable for cooking. Perfect choice!*

Apple-Sausage Breakfast Quiche

Makes a 9" (23 cm) quiche

Nestling sweet and savory flavors side-by-side makes each one even more noticeable, such as in this sweet-and-savory quiche featuring fresh apples and breakfast sausages. The cinnamon highlights the natural sweetness of the apple, and the eggs underscore the savoriness of the pork. Cooking the apples in almond oil provides a bonus hint of nuttiness. If you like, you can accentuate the almond flavor by drizzling more oil over each slice of quiche when you serve it. And if you're a big fan of sage, which is the primary herb used in breakfast-style sausages, feel free to whisk another teaspoon or two of dried sage into the milk and eggs. It's a natural fit.

Almond oil for cooking

3 large, firm apples such as Fuji or Gala, preferably organic

1 teaspoon cinnamon

½ pound (224 g) breakfast-link-style pork sausages

¾ cup (180 ml) whole milk*

6 eggs

Preheat the oven to 400°F (200°C) and grease a 9" (23 cm) pie pan.

In a large skillet, heat a generous drizzle of oil over medium-low heat. Cut the apples into thin slices—discarding the cores and stems—and place them in the skillet as you go. Stir in the cinnamon and cook, stirring occasionally, for 5 to 10 minutes over medium heat, or until the apple slices are starting to turn translucent but still feel firm when pressed with a spatula or wooden spoon. The more thinly the apples are sliced, the more quickly they'll cook.

Transfer the apples to a large mixing bowl. Add the sausages to the skillet the apples were in and sauté the sausage over medium-low heat for 3 to 5 minutes, occasionally rolling/flipping them to cook all sides evenly. Pre-cooked sausages only need a minute or two to brown; raw sausages will need at least 5 minutes to cook all the way through. Use the edge of a spatula to break the sausages into small pieces before transferring them from the pan to the bowl with the apples in it.

Whisk the milk and eggs into the apple and sausage mixture, and then pour everything into the prepared pie pan. Bake for 30 minutes, or until the top is golden-brown and slightly puffed. Let the quiche cool on a wire rack. You can serve the quiche chilled or warm.

Leftover quiche can be refrigerated for a week. Feel free to drizzle each serving with a splash of almond oil if you like!

*To make this dish Paleo-friendly, use whole coconut milk in place of dairy milk.

Near East Jeweled Pilaf with Lamb, Carrots and Sunchokes

Makes 4 servings

You might see a few new ingredients in this recipe: sunchokes, saffron and orange blossom water. The latter is easy to find in Middle Eastern grocery stores or in mainstream stores that boast well-stocked ethnic food sections, and you can usually find saffron in the spice aisle. Saffron lends both a yellow hue and its signature earthy flavor to the dish, but if you can't find saffron, you could add a dash of turmeric and/or sweet paprika to mimic the color (and, in the case of turmeric, the earthiness). Just be careful not to let any of those spices come into contact with countertops, clothing or anything porous because their hues are so vivid that they'll stain whatever they touch.

4 sunchokes (also called Jerusalem artichokes)
¾ cup (139 g) brown rice*
Pistachio oil for cooking
1 yellow onion, chopped
2 large carrots, scrubbed and chopped
4 dried apricots, chopped
10 pitted green olives, chopped
Pinch saffron
2 teaspoons (5 g) cumin
2 teaspoons (4 g) coriander
1 teaspoon cinnamon
½ teaspoon cardamom
Dash sea salt
1 pound (448 g) ground lamb
2 tablespoons (30 ml) orange blossom water or rosewater
¾ cup (131 g) pomegranate seeds
Whole-milk plain Greek yogurt for garnishing*

To prep the sunchokes, have a bowl of cool water ready. (Sunchokes turn brown fast.) Peel the chokes and cut them into 1" (2.5 cm) cubes, immediately dropping them into the water.

Fill a medium pot halfway with water and bring to a boil. Quickly drain the chokes, transfer them to the pot, and simmer them for 5 minutes, or until they are tender when pierced with a fork. Drain well.

In a medium pot, simmer the rice and 1½ cups (360 ml) water, covered, over low heat for 40 minutes, or until the rice has absorbed all of the water. Fluff with a fork and remove from the heat.

In a large skillet, heat the oil, onion and carrots over medium-low heat. Cook for 10 minutes, or until the onion is turning translucent. Stir in the apricots, olives, spices, lamb and orange blossom water and increase the heat to medium. Cook for 5 minutes, stirring often, or until the lamb is opaque all of the way through. Remove from the heat and stir in the pomegranate seeds, drained sunchokes and cooked rice. Serve immediately, garnishing each portion with a dollop of yogurt if you like.

Leftover pilaf can be refrigerated for 4 days.

To make this a Paleo-friendly dish, substitute 1 small head of cauliflower (florets only, coarsely chopped) for the rice. Simmer the cauliflower for 5 minutes and drain it well before stirring into the pilaf. Also, for a Paleo-friendly dish, omit the yogurt.

Lamb, Cashew and Sweet Potato Biryani with Pistachio Oil

Makes 4 servings

Of all of the nut oils, pistachio is perhaps the most intriguing. It's extremely aromatic and nutty, and it also has a very faint greenish hue, which makes it great for drizzling onto finished dishes. (It's also fantastic on vanilla ice cream!) It can handle medium-low heat, so you can use it for cooking, too. Pistachios originally hail from Central Asia and the Middle East, and they are often used in biryanis, which is the Indian version of pilaf. In this case, the ultra-nutty pistachio oil provides a contrast to the milder, almost sweet flavor of the cashews. Feel free to adjust the level of curry powder depending on your personal preference. Cooks unfamiliar with Indian–style dishes may wish to use less, while fans of turmeric (a key ingredient in curry powder) may want to add more.

2 large sweet potatoes, scrubbed and trimmed, cut into ¼" (0.6 cm) cubes
Coconut oil for tossing
Sea salt
Pistachio oil for cooking and drizzling
1 yellow onion, chopped
6 cloves garlic, chopped
1 cup (140 g) raw cashews, coarsely chopped
2 tablespoons (13 g) curry powder
2 teaspoons (4 g) ginger
1½ pounds (672 g) leg of lamb, trimmed and cut into ½" (1.2 cm-) thick strips
Juice of ½ lemon
1 small bunch cilantro, leaves only
Whole-milk plain Greek yogurt for garnishing*

Preheat the oven to 375°F (190°C) and line 2 baking sheets with parchment paper.

In a large bowl, toss the sweet potatoes with a generous spoonful of coconut oil and a dash of salt. Arrange the potatoes on the baking sheets so that none of the cubes overlap, and then roast them for 30 minutes, or until the potatoes are turning golden brown on the bottom.

In a large skillet, heat a drizzle of pistachio oil and the onion over medium-low heat. Cook for 5 minutes, or until the onion is turning translucent, and then stir in the garlic, cashews, curry powder, ginger and a dash of salt. Cook for an additional 5 minutes.

Stir in the lamb, lemon juice and cilantro and continue to cook for 8 minutes over medium-low heat, or until the lamb is done to your liking. (For medium-rare, it should be pink in the center; if you'd like it well done, it should be opaque when cut in half.) Stir in the roasted sweet potatoes, and then serve immediately, drizzling each portion with a little more pistachio oil and garnishing with a dollop of yogurt.

Leftover biryani can be refrigerated for 4 days.

To make this dish more Paleo-friendly, omit the yogurt.

Za'atar-Spiced Green Wraps with Chicken, Onions and Figs and Lentil-Yogurt Dip

Makes 4 servings

Za'atar is a popular spice blend in Middle Eastern kitchens. Home cooks often make their own, which is easy enough to do: Place 1 tablespoon (8 g) sesame seeds, 1½ teaspoons (1.5 g) oregano, 1½ teaspoons (1.5 g) thyme, ½ teaspoon sea salt, and 1 tablespoon (7 g) ground sumac in a clean spice jar and shake well. Store the unused portion in a cool, dark place for future use. Whisk some za'atar into extra-virgin olive oil and red wine vinegar to make a quick dressing for Greek salads, or stir it into plain whole-milk Greek yogurt or Coconut Cream (see page 111) to make an instant dip. Don't be shy! Think of za'atar as the Middle Eastern version of dried Italian seasoning.

FOR THE DIP

1 cup (240 ml) water
⅓ cup (64 g) brown lentils*
7 ounces (196 ml) whole-milk plain Greek yogurt**
2 teaspoons (5 g) cumin
Sea salt to taste

FOR THE FILLING AND WRAPS

8 large collard leaves, bottom 3" (7.5 cm) cut off and discarded
Generous drizzle pistachio oil for cooking and drizzling
2 large yellow onions, chopped
4 cloves garlic, chopped
4 fresh figs, each cut into 8 pieces
1 pound (448 g) chicken breast, cut into ½" (1.2 cm-) thick strips
1 tablespoon + 1 teaspoon (8 g) za'atar (See headnote for how to blend your own za'atar)

In a medium pot, bring the water to a boil. Stir in the lentils, and then reduce the heat to medium-low, and simmer for 20 to 25 minutes, or until the lentils have reached the desired tenderness. Drain well. Place the lentils in a food processor, add the remaining dip ingredients, and process until well blended. Set aside.

While the lentils simmer, fill a large pot with at least 4" (10 cm) of water and bring to a boil. Slide in the collard leaves and reduce the heat to medium. Simmer for 3 minutes, and then promptly remove the leaves with tongs and let them drain/cool in a colander.

In a large skillet, heat the oil and onions over medium-low heat. Cook for 10 minutes, stirring occasionally, or until the onions are turning translucent. Increase the heat to medium and add the remaining ingredients. Cook for 5 minutes, or until the thickest piece of chicken is opaque when cut in half, flipping the chicken halfway through the cooking time.

Spread a cooled collard leaf out on a plate or cutting board and place a spoonful of the chicken filling in the lower third of the leaf. If you like, add a dab of the dip, or reserve the dip for dipping. Drizzle with a little pistachio oil. Fold the bottom of the leaf up onto the filling. Fold in each edge of the leaf and then roll the leaf up, turning it over and tucking in the sides until the leaf is a neat package. Place seam-side down. Repeat with remaining leaves and filling and serve immediately.

*Lentils are not a Paleo ingredient, but they are an unprocessed, whole food.

**For a Paleo-friendly dish, use Coconut Cream (page 111) in place of the yogurt.

Salmon, Sesame and Avocado Sushi Bowls with Macadamia Nut Oil and Shredded Daikon

Makes 4 servings

If you don't have a rolling mat to make your sushi—or you're not particularly gifted at rolling—don't despair! You can lay out your ingredients rather than roll them. That's especially useful when your seaweed is no longer supple enough to roll (once you've opened a fresh package of nori, leftover sheets tend to get brittle and crack easily) or when you're feeling fumble-fingered. Or perhaps you just want something a little different. That's when you can make sushi bowls. All you have to do is arrange the ingredients on a plate—no rolling required. It doesn't get any simpler than that.

About 3 cups (558 g) cooked whole-grain sticky rice* (brown, red, purple or black)
Generous drizzle macadamia nut oil
1 red bell pepper, stem and seeds removed, flesh cut into thin slices
4 sheets nori, chopped or crumbled
2 green onions, green parts only, minced
1 avocado, flesh only, chopped
½ pound to ¾ pound (224 to 336 g) sashimi-grade raw salmon (called "sake" in Japanese)
1 daikon radish, peeled and grated or shredded
Toasted sesame seeds for garnishing

In a large bowl, toss together the rice, oil, pepper, nori and onions. Gently stir in the avocado. Spoon into 4 individual bowls and top each bowl with equal portions of the salmon and radish. Garnish with a sprinkling of sesame seeds.

*For a Paleo-friendly dish, substitute cauliflower for the rice. Run a small head of cauliflower—florets only—through a food processor until you have rice-sized pieces. Fill a large pot halfway with water and bring to a boil. Add the cauliflower and simmer for 3 to 5 minutes, or until cauliflower has reached the desired tenderness, and then drain well before using it in place of rice.

Citrusy Shrimp and Basil Spaghetti with Macadamia Oil

Makes 4 servings

Although you could make this dish during the winter months to lighten the mood, something about shrimp and basil shouts "It's summertime!" The fresh flavor of citrus and the rich, buttery undertone of macadamia nut oil add welcome accents, plus drizzling the spaghetti liberally with oil and citrus juice makes it easier to toss. If you can't find chives, you could garnish this dish with minced green onions instead, using only the green parts to keep their oniony flavor at a mild, chive-like level. Or you could use thinly sliced Vidalia onions for a sweeter garnish.

8 ounces (224 g) whole-grain gluten-free spaghetti*
Macadamia nut oil for cooking and drizzling
1½ pounds (672 g) wild-caught U.S. shrimp, peeled and deveined
Juice and zest of ½ lemon
Double handful macadamia nuts, chopped
Handful fresh basil leaves
Sea salt to taste
Freshly cracked black pepper to taste
Snipped chives for garnishing

Prepare the spaghetti according to the package directions. While it cooks, heat a drizzle of the oil in a large skillet over medium heat. Add the shrimp and cook for 3 to 4 minutes, flipping the shrimp after 2 minutes, or until the shrimp are curled and opaque all the way through. Immediately remove the shrimp to a plate. If you like, cut the shrimp into smaller pieces.

In a bowl, toss the cooked spaghetti and shrimp with lemon juice, lemon zest, another drizzle of oil and the nuts.

Roll the basil leaves into a tight tube and cut them into thin slices. Toss the basil ribbons into the pasta and add salt and pepper it to taste. Finish by garnishing each serving with the chives. Because basil blackens quickly when cut, it's best to enjoy this dish right away.

*For a Paleo-friendly dish, use spiralized zucchini noodles in place of the spaghetti.

Slow-Cooked Shredded Pork with Pineapple, Lime and Macadamia Salsa and Sweet Potato Crisps

Makes 4 servings

Not all salsas are tomato-based, as you can see from this recipe. Classic salsa verde, or green salsa, doesn't contain tomatoes, either. It's based on tomatillos. Because the term "salsa" simply means "sauce," salsa can be whatever you want it to be. In this recipe, the sweet pineapples and red bell peppers contrast nicely with the savory slow-cooked pork. Hawaiians have been making pineapple-and-pork dishes for as long as pigs have been on the islands, and they've long been harvesting macadamia nuts and enjoying their luscious oil, too. This recipe puts all three of those ingredients to delicious use.

FOR THE PORK

3 pounds (1.3 kg) pork butt (bone in or bone removed), if necessary cut into pieces to fit into the slow cooker
1 yellow onion, chopped
6 cloves garlic, chopped
2 tablespoons (15 g) chili powder
1 tablespoon (6 g) coriander
4 cups (960 ml) chicken broth

FOR THE SALSA

1 small pineapple, trimmed and cored, flesh cut into ½" (1.2 cm) cubes
1 red bell pepper, seeds and stem removed, chopped
Small bunch cilantro, leaves only, chopped
Several slices red onion, minced
½ cup (68 g) roasted macadamias, chopped
Juice of ½ lime

FOR THE CRISPS

Macadamia nut oil for cooking
2 sweet potatoes, scrubbed and trimmed, cut into very thin slices
Sea salt for sprinkling

Place the pork, onion, garlic, chili powder and coriander in a 6-quart (5.7 L) slow cooker. Pour in the broth and cook on high for 6 hours. (The meat should start to fall away from the bone when you lift it up.)

Turn off the cooker and pull out the meat with tongs. Let the pork cool until you can comfortably touch it. Use your fingertips (or two forks) to pull the pork away from the bone, and then pull/shred the meat into bite-sized pieces. If you're not going to use it all, you might want to leave the leftover meat as hunks rather than shredded. That way, the leftover meat will be moister.

In a glass mixing bowl, combine all of the salsa ingredients and toss well. Set aside.

Coat the bottom of a large skillet with the oil and place over medium heat. Add the potatoes, arranging them so that they don't overlap. You'll need to do this in several batches. As soon as the oil starts to sizzle, cook the potatoes for 6 minutes, flipping them halfway through, or until the potatoes are starting to turn golden brown on both sides.

Transfer the crisps to a plate covered with paper towels. Sprinkle the crisps with salt. With each batch of potatoes, you might need to cook them for less time since the pan will be hotter, or reduce the heat slightly. Serve the potatoes alongside the shredded pork and salsa.

Roasted Chicken with Kale, Beet and Cranberry Salad

Makes 4 servings, plus leftover roasted chicken

Roasting a chicken is shockingly simple, albeit a lost art. The secret? Use a rack, preferably the kind that allows you to stand the chicken upright. Because the drippings will run off of the chicken as it roasts, place the rack in a deep-rimmed pan to catch the lovely schmaltz, and then toss the schmaltz with anything you like (such as the Old-Fashioned Potato Salad on page 144) to create a richly flavored dressing.

CHICKEN
4 pounds (1.8 kg) whole chicken
Sea salt
Black pepper

SALAD
½ red onion, sliced thinly
3 medium beets, peeled and trimmed, cut into ½" (1.2 cm) cubes
1 large bunch kale, tough stems torn away, leaves roughly chopped
Pecan oil for cooking and drizzling
Double handful fresh cranberries (or a single handful unsweetened dried cranberries)
About 20 fresh sage leaves
Salt to taste
Roasted pumpkin seeds for garnishing

Preheat the oven to 375°F (190°C) and position a wire rack over a deep rectangular metal baking pan. Rinse the chicken well and pat it dry. Use kitchen shears to snip off the extra skin at both ends of the chicken. Snip off the tailbone, too, and discard it. Hold up the chicken and sprinkle it liberally with salt and pepper.

Place the chicken on the rack on its "back" with its "arms" and "legs" poking straight up. Or use a stand-up rack to impale the chicken on the rack. Roast for 1¾ hours, or until the chicken is a deep golden brown, and an inserted meat thermometer reads 180°F (82°C).

Let the chicken stand for at least 10 minutes before carving it. Be sure to pour the drippings into a clean glass jar. The drippings are delicious schmaltz! You can thin the drippings with a little red wine for an amazingly rich gravy, whisk the drippings into everything from soups to sauces (so much better than bouillon!), or smear the drippings onto bread in lieu of butter.

While the chicken roasts, soak the onion in a bowl of cool water to give it a milder, more mellow flavor. Rinse and drain the onion well. Fill a medium pot halfway with water and bring to a boil. Add the beets, reduce the heat to medium and simmer for 10 minutes. Drain well.

Meanwhile, in a large skillet, cook the kale with about 2 tablespoons (30 ml) water. Cover and cook over medium heat for about 5 minutes to wilt the kale. Uncover and continue to cook, stirring often, for another minute, or until the water has completely evaporated and the kale is soft. Turn off the heat and stir in the drained beets, a generous drizzle of the oil and the cranberries. Transfer everything to a large bowl and toss with the drained onions.

Wipe out the skillet and add a thin layer of oil and the sage leaves. Cook over medium-low heat for 3 minutes, or until the leaves are bubbling and starting to turn golden brown. Place them on paper towels to drain, and then crumble them into the salad. Toss well and season to taste with salt. Garnish the salad with the pumpkin seeds and serve it alongside the roasted chicken.

Pecan-Parmesan Crisps with Italian Herbs

Makes 4 side servings

Ever seen fancy Parmesan crisps sold in stores and wondered how to make them? It's simple: Melt grated Parmesan in a skillet and cook until the cheese begins to turn golden brown and is hard enough to flip. It can't get any easier than that! In this recipe, you'll mix the Parmesan with Italian herbs and cook it with a hint of pecan oil, but feel free to use whatever herbs and oil you like best. (Just don't use a polyunsaturated oil such as walnut or flaxseed because those should never be heated.) Crisps make great snacks, or you can crumble them to use them in place of croutons or corn chips. Whenever you want a crunchy garnish, make Parmesan crisps!

1 cup (100 g) grated Parmesan-Reggiano*
2 teaspoons (3 g) dried Italian herbs
Pecan oil for cooking and garnishing

In a medium bowl, toss the Parmesan with the herbs.

In a large skillet, drizzle 4 puddles of oil, and then carefully sprinkle ¼ cup (25 g) of the Parmesan mixture onto each puddle to make 4 mounds. Cook over medium-low heat for 5 to 7 minutes, or until the crisps are bubbling, turning brown around the edges, and have become firm enough to gently flip. Continue to cook the crisps for an additional minute to brown the other side, and then promptly remove them from the heat. Drizzle the crisps with additional pecan oil before serving.

*Cheese isn't a Paleo ingredient, but imported Parmesan-Reggiano made from raw milk from grass-fed cows is closer to Paleo concepts than conventional cheeses are.

Pear, Sage and Cheddar Frittata with Pecan Oil

Makes 4 servings

The French call it an omelet, the Spanish call it a tortilla and the Italians call it a frittata. You'll call it delicious. This recipe is essentially a thick omelet replete with sage, Cheddar and pear. It's savory and sweet in the same skillet. It's customizable, too, because you can swap out the pears for apples, the Cheddar for feta and the sage for basil. Or opt for whatever kinds of fruits, cheeses and herbs you like. Pretty much any combination you choose will pair beautifully with the buttery pecan oil. It's okay to cut the frittata into pieces to flip it, because even if you can see faint seams after you've finished cooking the frittata, you can use them as guidelines when you cut it into pieces. The thin pear slices will give each portion an elegant look.

1 sweet onion, thinly sliced
Pecan oil for cooking
6 eggs
2 tablespoons (3 g) dried sage
Generous grind black pepper
2 cups (225 g) grated Cheddar*
1 Bosc pear, core and stem removed, flesh cut into thin slices

In a large skillet, cook the onion in a generous drizzle of the oil over medium heat for 15 minutes, stirring occasionally, or until the onion is soft and translucent.

While the onion cooks, in a large bowl, whisk together the remaining ingredients, and then whisk in the cooked onion.

Pour another drizzle of oil into the same skillet (no need to clean!) and add the egg mixture. Cover and cook for 10 minutes over medium-low heat.

To flip the frittata, cut it into quarters and carefully flip over each quarter. Cover again and cook for 8 minutes or until both sides are golden brown. If you want a particularly beautiful golden-brown frittata, hold a large plate over the skillet and turn the skillet over, allowing the frittata to fall onto the plate. Slide the frittata back into the skillet and continue to cook for another 2 minutes to achieve a more pronounced browning effect. Slide the frittata onto a large plate and serve immediately.

Leftover frittata can be refrigerated for 5 days.

*Cheese isn't a Paleo ingredient, but raw Cheddar from grass-fed cows is closer to Paleo concepts than conventional cheeses are.

Recipes with Polyunsaturated Fats: A Delicate Touch

Flaxseed Oil, Walnut Oil, Sesame Oil, Pumpkin Seed Oil

Most polyunsaturated oils are seed oils, including flaxseed oil, walnut oil, sesame oil and pumpkin seed oil. Often those seeds are roasted before they're pressed for their oil. (Walnut oil, the nutty exception to the seed rule, is also sometimes made from roasted walnuts.) Roasting the entire seed results in a toasty, flavorful oil that ranges in hue from honey-golden to warm maroon-orange.

Even though you shouldn't cook with most polyunsaturated oils—pumpkin seed oil and sesame seed oil are the only varieties that can handle any heat at all, and even then only very low heat—there are plenty of opportunities to use these oils, from drizzles to dips to dressings. Or host an oil tasting! The rich and unique qualities of polyunsaturated oils make them party favorites.

To lengthen the life of these delicate oils, remember that all polyunsaturated oils should be stored in the refrigerator (even before they're opened). And remember that walnut oil, flaxseed oil, hemp seed oil and squash seed oils should never be heated. That's because those oils are even higher in polyunsaturated fats than pumpkin seed and sesame seed oils are. You can, however, use polyunsaturated oils to garnish finished dishes, baked goods and even ice cream. Keep reading to get more delicious ideas!

Recipe notes: A "drizzle" of oil means about 1 tablespoon (15 ml).

All herbs are dried unless listed as fresh.

Roasted Pork Tenderloin with Scandinavian Beet, Carrot and Apple Slaw

Makes 4 servings

Thanks to its high levels of anti-inflammatory omega-3 fats, flaxseed oil is the most well-known member of the polyunsaturated family. It's also the easiest one to find. Look for it in refrigerated cases in health-oriented grocery stores. The grassy, vegetal notes of flaxseed oil give it a pronounced flavor, which means it pairs well with a medley of veggies and fruits. Bold herbs such as dill also pair well with the forward nature of flaxseed oil. If you'd like to allow the flavor of flaxseed oil to shine through more, drizzle it onto flatbreads in place of butter or make a simple pasta dish with flaxseed oil, fresh herbs and lots of thinly sliced summery vegetables, such as peppers, carrots and zucchini. Or use this flax-and-dill dressing for any salad you like.

FOR THE PORK
Generous knob of ghee
1 pound (448 g) pork tenderloin, rinsed and patted dry
Dry red wine or water for deglazing

FOR THE DRESSING
¼ cup (60 ml) flaxseed oil
2 tablespoons (30 ml) apple cider vinegar
1 teaspoon dill
Sea salt to taste
Freshly ground pepper to taste

FOR THE SLAW
¼ head of cabbage, thinly sliced
1 large carrot, scrubbed and grated
2 beets, washed, peeled, and grated
1 large, firm apple
Sprig fresh dill for garnish (optional)

Preheat the oven to 350°F (180°C).

In a large skillet, melt the ghee over medium heat. Add the pork and cook just until the pork is browning, about 4 minutes per side. You'll still have two "sides" that aren't browned, so roll the tenderloin over to one of the sides and hold it in place for 1 minute to brown. Repeat with the final "side." Transfer the pork to an 8" x 8" (20 cm x 20 cm) baking dish.

Add a drizzle of wine or water to the skillet and reduce the heat to medium-low. Gently loosen the drippings on the bottom of the skillet and pour the drippings over the pork. Bake the tenderloin for 20 minutes (for medium-rare) or 25 minutes (for medium), or until the internal temperature of the pork has reached 145°F (63°C). Let the pork stand for 10 minutes before slicing. If you like, add another knob of ghee to the pan as the pork is resting—that will create a thicker sauce.

While the pork roasts, make the dressing and slaw.

In a small bowl, whisk together the oil, vinegar, dill, salt and pepper and set aside.

In a bowl, toss the cabbage, carrot and beets together. Cut the apple into thin matchsticks, and then add it to the bowl with the veggies. Pour on the dressing and toss well to coat. The apple cider vinegar will prevent the cut apple from turning brown.

Serve the slaw with the sliced pork, garnishing the slaw with a fresh sprig of dill if you like.

Leftover pork and slaw can be refrigerated for 3 days.

Beef, Arugula and Broccoli with Flaxseed Oil

Makes 4 servings

Before Chez Panisse ushered in the modern age of microgreens and sourcing produce from local farmers, American shoppers didn't have much choice when it came to lettuce. There was iceberg, Romaine, and if you were particularly lucky, leaf lettuce. But now grocery stores devote entire sections to lettuce in all of its various forms. Arugula (called "rocket" in Europe) falls into the peppery/bitter category when it comes to greens, which makes it hearty and flavorful enough to be sautéed and included in a savory beef dish like this. Other peppery/bitter greens include watercress, mizuna and tatsoi. You could also use baby spinach in place of the arugula, although the baby spinach isn't quite as peppery.

1 head broccoli, florets only
Extra-virgin olive oil for cooking
½ red onion, thinly sliced
1½ pounds (672 g) top sirloin, trimmed and cut into ½" (1.2 cm-) thick strips
2 tablespoons (30 ml) apple cider vinegar
12 leaves fresh basil, rolled into tight cylinders and then cut into thin strips (a.k.a. "chiffonade")
10 ounces (280 g) arugula leaves
Dash sea salt
¼ cup (36 g) toasted sunflower seeds
1 firm apple, such as Gala, core and stem removed, flesh cut into thin slices*
Flaxseed oil for drizzling

Fill a large pot halfway with water and bring to a boil. Add the broccoli and simmer for 5 minutes. Drain well.

In a large skillet, heat a generous splash of olive oil over medium-low heat. Add the onion and beef and cook for 5 minutes, flipping the beef halfway through, or until the beef has reached the desired doneness. Add the vinegar, basil, arugula and salt and continue to cook for another minute or two, stirring often, or just until the arugula has begun to wilt.

Remove the skillet from the heat and stir in the sunflower seeds and apples, and then drizzle with flaxseed oil.

Leftover beef can be refrigerated for 3 days. You might want to add the apples to individual portions rather than tossing them into the mix if you think you'll have leftovers, because even though you're tossing the apple slices with vinegar, they'll still turn brown after a few hours.

*To prevent the apple slices from browning, place them in a bowl with cold water and a drizzle of the vinegar. Briefly drain the apples before adding them to the beef.

Zucchini and Yellow Tomato Gazpacho with Crisped Prosciutto

Makes 4 servings

Cold soups such as gazpacho, cucumber soup and fruit soup are excellent dishes to make when you want to showcase delicate oils like flaxseed, which should never be heated. The summery sweetness of ripe tomatoes and peppers contrasts deliciously with the grassy, fresh flavor of flaxseed oil, and the ultra-savory character of prosciutto provides an unusual counterpoint. Imported Parma prosciutto is made with hams from pastured hogs. Its flavor is distinctly stronger than that of domestic hams, and so a little goes a long way. Lightly cooking the prosciutto makes it crispy, like a strip of bacon, and infuses the gazpacho with a burst of texture along with flavor. When buying prosciutto, be sure to ask for it to be thinly sliced.

2 pounds (896 g) large yellow tomatoes, stems discarded

1 yellow pepper, seeds and stem removed

1 zucchini, ends trimmed

2 cloves garlic

2 tablespoons (30 ml) sherry or red wine vinegar

1 teaspoon sea salt

2 tablespoons (30 ml) flaxseed oil

½ cup (86 g) cooked white beans*

½ pound (224 g) Parma prosciutto, thinly sliced

Cut the tomatoes, pepper and zucchini into rough chunks and place them in a food processor. Add all of the other ingredients except the prosciutto and blend until you have a chunky soup. This works particularly well if you have a high-speed blender like a Vitamix.

To crisp the prosciutto, place as many slices as you can comfortably fit (without overlapping them) in a large skillet. Cook over medium-low heat for 2 minutes, or until the slices are turning crisp and light brown. Coarsely chop them and sprinkle each serving of gazpacho with the prosciutto.

Leftover gazpacho can be refrigerated for 3 days.

*For a Paleo-friendly dish, omit the beans.

> **Tip:** *Hemp seed oil can be tricky to find, so it isn't featured in this book. It is, however, interchangeable with flaxseed oil, so if you find hemp seed oil, use it in similar ways.*

Strawberry-Maple Ice Cream
with Toasted Coconut and Walnut Oil

Makes about 4 cups (544 g) ice cream

An ice cream maker might be the best single-purpose kitchen appliance you ever buy. Grass-fed milk and cream (or coconut milk and cream) make deliciously nutritious ice cream compared with store-bought brands made with conventional dairy products. You can skip white sugar in favor of sweeteners such as fruit, maple syrup and/or honey. Just bear in mind that homemade ice cream tends to crystallize when frozen for more than a day or two. Adding high-proof alcohol helps lower the freezing point of the ice cream, which prevents that rock-solid hardness. Or let the ice cream sit at room temperature for 20 minutes before serving it.

FOR THE ICE CREAM

1 cup (240 ml) heavy cream*

1 cup (240 ml) half-and-half*

4 egg yolks

⅓ cup (80 ml) maple syrup

16 ounces (448 g) fresh strawberries, rinsed and drained

1 shot good-quality, unflavored vodka or rum (Optional, but see headnote)

1 teaspoon almond or vanilla extract

FOR THE TOPPINGS

½ cup (43 g) unsweetened coconut flakes

Walnut oil for drizzling

Place all of the ice cream ingredients in a blender except for the vodka and extract and blend until velvety smooth. Transfer the mixture to a medium pot.

Heat the mixture on medium-low for 3 minutes, whisking occasionally. When tiny bubbles form, continue to cook gently for another 5 minutes, whisking more often and keeping a close eye on it. You don't want it to come to a full simmer since that could overcook the egg yolks and make your ice cream chunky.

Remove the mixture from the heat and pour it into a cool bowl. Whisk in the vodka and extract. Taste it to see if you'd like your ice cream to be sweeter; if so, add a touch more maple syrup. Wait for the cream to cool. If you want to cool the cream quickly, fill a larger bowl with ice water and place the bowl with the ice cream inside the larger bowl, being careful not to get any water into the cream. Whisk for several minutes to rapidly chill the cream, testing occasionally to see if it's chilled yet.

When the mixture is completely cool, place it in an ice cream maker and follow the manufacturer instructions.

Freeze the churned ice cream in small containers. Headroom will make the ice cream crystallize all the more quickly, and you don't want that.

In a large skillet, toast the coconut over medium heat for 3 minutes, stirring the flakes occasionally, or until the coconut is fragrant and turning golden brown. Remove the toasted flakes to a cool plate. Serve the ice cream topped with the toasted coconut and a generous drizzling of the walnut oil.

*To make this dish Paleo-friendly, use Coconut Cream (see page 111) in place of the dairy cream and unsweetened whole coconut milk in place of the half-and-half.

Chicken, Asparagus and Egg Salad with Walnut Ranch Dressing and Avocado

Makes 4 servings

For decades, America's favorite dressing has been Ranch. Originally, Ranch was based on buttermilk and fresh herbs, but now the commercially bottled version relies on heavily refined oils such as soybean and canola. Here's your chance to remake the national dressing in a fresh new way! Thinning yogurt with lemon juice provides a buttermilk-like consistency, and adding a touch of walnut oil provides a smooth, nutty (and anti-inflammatory!) accent that partners beautifully with chicken and asparagus. Use this dressing for dips, garnishes and even as a condiment. You can't go wrong with upgraded Ranch.

FOR THE DRESSING

¼ cup (58 g) plain whole-milk Greek yogurt*
2 teaspoons (10 ml) fresh lemon juice
2 teaspoons (2 g) minced chives
1 teaspoon dill
1 tablespoon (15 ml) walnut oil
Sea salt to taste
Ground pepper to taste

FOR THE SALAD

4 eggs
½ pound (224 g) asparagus, woody ends snapped off and discarded
Extra-virgin olive oil for cooking
1 pound (448 g) boneless skinless chicken breasts, cut into bite-sized pieces
1 avocado, flesh only, cubed
8 leaves Romaine, rinsed well, patted dry, and chopped
1 cup (130 g) frozen green peas, thawed
Handful walnuts, chopped

In a small bowl, whisk together the dressing ingredients. If the dressing is too thick to pour, add another teaspoon of walnut oil and whisk again. Refrigerate until needed.

In a medium pot, submerge the eggs in water. Bring to boil. As soon as the water starts to boil, reduce the heat to low, cover the pot and cook the eggs for 10 minutes. Immediately run cold water into the pot to cool the pot and the eggs, and then let the eggs sit in the cold water for a few minutes before peeling and chopping them.

While the eggs cook, fill a wide but shallow pot halfway with water and bring to a boil. Add the asparagus and cook for 3 minutes *only*. Immediately drain the asparagus. Let it sit in cold water for a few minutes, and then drain the asparagus well and cut it into bite-sized pieces.

In a large skillet, heat a generous drizzle of extra-virgin olive oil over medium heat. Add the chicken and cook, flipping it occasionally, for 5 minutes, or until the thickest piece is opaque when cut in half.

Transfer the cooked chicken to a large bowl and add the chopped asparagus, chopped eggs and remaining ingredients. Toss well. Add the dressing and toss again, and then serve immediately.

If you think you may have leftovers, dress each salad individually. Undressed salad can be refrigerated for 3 days, and the dressing can be refrigerated for 1 week.

To make this dish Paleo-friendly, use Coconut Cream (see page 111) in place of the yogurt.

Spinach, Apple and Green Bean Toss with Roasted Chicken and Balsamic-Walnut Dressing

Makes 4 servings

Using walnut oil as the base for salad dressings is a great way to give it a chance to truly shine. Walnut's rich, buttery flavor complements everything from fruit and greens to chicken and fish—or pretty much anything else, for that matter. Because walnut oil is free-flowing right out of the refrigerator, all you have to do to make a luscious dressing is shake the walnut oil in a small jar with some balsamic vinegar and sea salt. If you'd like to play with your walnut-based dressings, try adding a dollop of stone-ground mustard, a spoonful of whole-milk plain Greek yogurt and/or some dried Italian herbs. The possibilities are endless! And they're so easy, too.

FOR THE DRESSING

¼ cup (60 ml) walnut oil
2 tablespoons (30 ml) balsamic vinegar
½ teaspoon sea salt

FOR THE SALAD

½ pound (224 g) green beans, trimmed and cut into bite-sized pieces
¼ red onion, thinly sliced*
5 ounces (140 g) baby spinach, washed and dried
4 ounces (112 g) blue cheese**
¾ to 1 pound (336 g to 448 g) roasted chicken breast, cut into ½" (1.2 cm-) wide strips (See page 186)
1 large apple, unpeeled and cut into thin slices
Handful fresh red currants or nonsugared dried cherries

Place all of the dressing ingredients in a screw-top jar, close tightly, and shake well.

Fill a medium pot halfway with water and bring to a boil. Add the green beans, reduce the heat to medium and simmer for 3 minutes. Drain well.

In a large bowl, toss together the cooked green beans with the remaining salad ingredients. Toss well. Drizzle on the dressing and toss well again before serving. Once the dressing is tossed with the salad, serve it immediately.

If you'd like your onion to be milder, soak the onion slices in cold water for at least 30 minutes before using, and then drain well.

**For a Paleo-friendly dish, omit the cheese.*

Sesame Beef Medallions, Asparagus, Ginger and Garlic with Toasted Sesame Oil

Makes 4 servings

Here's an opportunity to experience sesame oil two ways: as raw oil and as toasted oil. The latter is made by first toasting the seeds before pressing them for their oil, which makes a nuttier, deeper-tasting oil. Although you can use it for low-heat cooking, it's best as a finishing oil. But remember that a little goes a long way! If you prefer a milder effect, you can use the untoasted oil instead. Either way, the flavor of sesame lends an exotic flair to the asparagus and beef, plus it's a natural fit with Asian seasonings such as tamari and ginger. Remember to keep both kinds of sesame oil in the refrigerator.

3 tablespoons (24 g) sesame seeds, raw or toasted

1½ pounds (672 g) beef tenderloin, cut into 1" (2.5-cm) thick medallions

1 pound (448 g) asparagus

2 yellow squashes, ends trimmed, thinly sliced

Sesame oil for cooking

4 cloves garlic, thinly sliced

1 tablespoon (15 ml) rice wine vinegar*

1 teaspoon ginger

2 tablespoons (30 ml) gluten-free tamari, divided*

Toasted sesame oil for garnishing

Spread the sesame seeds out on a large plate. Press each medallion into the seeds, turning to coat each medallion. (Add more sesame seeds if necessary.) Set aside.

Rinse the asparagus and snap off the woody ends. Cover the bottom of a large skillet with water and bring to a boil. Add the asparagus, reduce heat to medium-low, and cover. Steam the stalks for 3 minutes, then promptly drain them and plunge the asparagus into ice water to cool it quickly. Drain again.

Place the squashes in a large skillet with a generous drizzle of the sesame oil. Cook over medium-low heat for 10 minutes or until the squash is starting to turn translucent. Stir in the garlic, vinegar, ginger and 1 tablespoon (15 ml) of the tamari and continue to cook for 5 minutes or until the garlic is soft and fragrant. Stir in a drizzle of the toasted sesame oil and the drained asparagus and remove from the heat. Cover to keep warm while you cook the beef.

Add another drizzle of the sesame oil to another large skillet and use tongs to transfer the medallions to the skillet. Cook over medium-low heat for 3 minutes, then add the remaining tablespoon (15 ml) of tamari and gently flip over the medallions with the tongs. Cook another 2 minutes, then cover and cook for a final 3 minutes or until the medallions have reached their desired doneness. Serve the medallions with a side of the asparagus and squash.

*To make this dish more Paleo-friendly, use lime juice in place of the rice wine vinegar and coconut aminos in place of the tamari.

White Tuna Sautéed with Mango, Mushrooms and Bok Choy

Makes 4 servings

White tuna is albacore tuna, but fresh filets taste very different from canned albacore. Grocery stores specializing in sushi ingredients (typically Japanese grocery stores) carry sashimi-grade white tuna, ahi tuna, salmon, etc. Sashimi-grade means you can consume the fish raw because it's very fresh and of very high quality. It's also ideal for low-heat cooking. If you can't find sashimi-grade white tuna, go with ahi or salmon—those will also be perfectly suited to minimal cooking. If you do find the white tuna, though, you'll be amazed at how creamy it tastes. It's the butter of the seas!

Sesame oil for cooking

1 pound (448 g) cremini or button mushrooms, cleaned and sliced

1 standard mango or 2 champagne mangoes, cut into ½" (1.2 cm) cubes

2 heads baby bok choy, bottom white stems cut away and discarded, leaves roughly chopped

6 green onions, green part only, minced

2 tablespoons (30 ml) wheat-free tamari, divided*

1½ pounds (672 g) sashimi-grade white tuna, cut into ½" (1.2 cm)-thick medallions

Toasted sesame oil for garnishing if desired

Pour a generous drizzle of sesame oil into a large skillet over medium-low heat. Add the mushrooms. As soon as the mushrooms start to sizzle, cook them for 10 minutes, stirring occasionally. Stir in the mango, bok choy, green onions and 1 tablespoon (15 ml) of the tamari. Cover and cook for 10 minutes or until the bok choy is wilted.

Remove the veggies to a warm dish and cover to keep warm. Return the skillet to the heat and add another drizzle of the sesame oil and the remaining tablespoon (15 ml) of tamari. Arrange the tuna medallions in the skillet so they don't overlap (cook them in batches if necessary) and cook for 5 minutes over medium-low heat, gently flipping each medallion over halfway through the cooking time. The medallions will be so tender after 5 minutes that you'll be able to cut them in half as easily as you can cut grass-fed butter.

Serve the medallions with a side of the veggies, garnishing with the toasted sesame oil if you like. Leftover veggies can be refrigerated for 4 days, but the tuna should be enjoyed within a day.

To make this dish more Paleo-friendly, use coconut aminos in place of the tamari.

Tip: *Make sure you buy polyunsaturated oils from stores with good turnover. Ideally, stores should store these oils in refrigerated cases, but at the very least, choose oils that are not sitting on a top shelf under bright, hot lights. Check the bottles for expiration dates and avoid bottles that are dusty.*

Gingered Shrimp, Green Bean and Broccoli Stir-Fry

Makes 4 servings

When shopping for shrimp, it's worth looking for U.S.–caught wild shrimp. Not only are they considered to be more sustainable than farmed shrimp from Southeast Asia, which are often raised in open systems that discharge concentrated waste products into the ocean, shrimp caught in the Gulf of Mexico tastes sweeter and more flavorful than farmed shrimp. And for the record, in the United States, shrimp and prawns are the same thing. The only difference is that the typical "prawn" is larger than the typical "shrimp." In Europe, larger-sized prawns are more common than smaller-sized shrimp, so you'll come across the term prawn more often. But shrimp and prawns are equally delicious!

1 pound (448 g) green beans, trimmed
1 head broccoli, florets only
2 tablespoons (32 ml) gluten-free miso*
3" (7.5 cm-) piece of ginger root, peeled and minced
¼ cup (60 ml) rice wine vinegar*
1 bunch chives, minced
Sesame oil for cooking
1½ pounds (672 g) wild-caught U.S. shrimp, peeled and deveined

Fill a large pot halfway with water and bring to a boil. Add the green beans and broccoli and simmer for 5 minutes. Drain well.

In a large skillet, cook the miso, ginger root, vinegar and chives in a generous drizzle of sesame oil over medium-low heat for 10 minutes. Stir in the shrimp and cook for 10 minutes, flipping over the shrimp halfway through, or until the shrimp are curled and opaque when cut in half. Stir in the drained beans and broccoli and serve immediately. Leftover shrimp can be refrigerated for 2 days.

To make this dish Paleo-friendly, use coconut aminos in place of the miso and apple cider vinegar rather than rice wine vinegar.

Crustless Chocolate Custard Flan Topped with Fresh Fruit and Pumpkin Seed Oil

Makes a 9" (23 cm) flan

When you hear the word "flan," you might think of a plain unadorned custard-style cake, or you might think of crusted cake with gorgeously arranged fruit on top. This version falls somewhere in between: Yes, it's a custard (albeit one infused with cocoa and maple), but it's also topped with fruit. Of course, flans typically aren't drizzled with rich-tasting oils, but why shouldn't they be? Desserts are ideal dishes for showcasing oils that shouldn't be heated. The full nutty flavor of pumpkin seed oil pairs beautifully with fruit and freshly whipped cream. Or use another no-heat nutty-tasting oil, like walnut or butternut squash seed oil.

6 eggs
⅓ cup (80 ml) maple syrup
¼ cup (16 g) unsweetened cocoa powder, preferably non–Dutched
Dash sea salt
2½ cups (600 g) whole milk*
1 teaspoon vanilla
At least 16 ounces (448 g) fresh fruit, either left whole if they're small (like blueberries) or sliced if the fruit is larger (like peaches, nectarines or strawberries)
Pumpkin seed oil for drizzling
Freshly whipped cream for garnishing, optional*

Preheat the oven to 325°F (170°C). Use a glass 9" (23 cm) pan that's at least 3" (7.5 cm) deep and grease it well. You'll need to be able to set this pan inside of a larger baking dish to make a water bath. In a large bowl, whisk the eggs, maple syrup, cocoa powder and salt until well blended. Set aside.

Place the milk in a medium pot and heat on high until just steaming, whisking occasionally. Slowly pour the hot milk into the egg mixture, whisking constantly. Whisk in the vanilla and pour the mixture into the greased pan.

Place the pan in a large glass baking dish and fill the outer dish with at least an inch (2.5 cm) of water, creating a water bath. Pull out the oven rack and carefully place the water-filled dish in the oven. Bake for 75 to 90 minutes or until the center is firm and set.

Carefully remove the flan from the water bath and let it cool on a wire rack. Top it with fresh fruit and a generous drizzle of pumpkin seed oil. Serve it with freshly whipped cream if you like.

For a Paleo-friendly dish, use whole unsweetened coconut milk in place of the dairy milk. Likewise, chill Coconut Cream (see page 111) and then whip that to use in place of whipped dairy cream.

Chili-Spiced Pork Medallions and Simmered Squash with Pumpkin Seed Oil

Makes 4 servings

Pumpkin seed oil is one of the most flavorful, nutty-tasting oils you'll ever come across—just one taste of it will make you think of Halloween and freshly roasted pumpkin seeds. Long popular in Austrian cuisine, pumpkin seed oil is now being produced in the Finger Lakes region of New York. A company called Stony Brook makes several varieties of squash seed oils, from delicata to acorn to kabocha seed oils, along with pumpkin and butternut squash seed oils. If you happen to have any butternut squash oil on hand, that would be another nice oil to use in this recipe.

FOR THE SQUASH

3 cups (720 ml) chicken broth or water (chicken broth will give the veggies more flavor)
1 small butternut squash, skin trimmed away and seeds removed, flesh cut into 1" (2.5 cm) cubes
1 pound (448 g) green beans, trimmed
1 tablespoon (3 g) oregano
Sea salt for sprinkling
Pumpkin seed oil for drizzling

FOR THE PORK MEDALLIONS

Extra-virgin olive oil for cooking
1 yellow onion, chopped
1½ pounds (672 g) pork tenderloin, trimmed and cut into 1" (2.5 cm)-thick slices
1 tablespoon (7 g) chili powder
1 tablespoon (7 g) cumin
Cherry tomatoes for garnishing, cut in half
Roasted pumpkin seeds for garnishing
Plain whole-milk Greek yogurt* (optional)

Pour the broth into a large pot. Bring to a boil and add the butternut squash. Simmer for 7 minutes, then add the green beans and continue to cook for an additional 3 minutes. Drain well. Transfer the veggies to a large bowl and toss them with the oregano, sea salt and pumpkin seed oil.

In a large skillet, heat the extra-virgin olive oil over medium heat. Add the onion and cook for 7 minutes, stirring often, or until the onion is fragrant and turning golden brown. Reduce the heat to medium-low and arrange the pork medallions in the skillet so that they don't overlap. Dust with the chili powder and cumin. Cook for 5 minutes uncovered, flipping the medallions over halfway through, then cover and continue to cook for another 7 minutes, again flipping halfway through, or until medallions have reached their desired doneness.

Garnish the medallions with tomatoes, pumpkin seeds and yogurt if you like. Serve with a side of the squash. Leftover pork and salad can be refrigerated for 4 days.

*For a Paleo-friendly dish, omit the yogurt.

Tip: *Butternut squash seed oil is another hard-to-find oil, so again, it isn't featured in this book. But it's similar in flavor to pumpkin seed oil, although more buttery in nature. Also remember not to heat butternut squash seed oil at all since it contains more polyunsaturated fat than pumpkin seed oil does. Butternut squash seed oil is an amazingly rich finishing oil to use in a variety of sweet and savory dishes. So are acorn squash seed oil and kabocha seed oil.*

Crab and Corn Gumbo

Makes 4 to 6 servings

Mardi Gras. New Orleans. Gumbo. You can't think of one without the other. This New Orleans classic has its origins in African cookery, which makes hearty use of okra, tomatoes and spices. The okra is an essential ingredient in the dish. In fact, many people think of "okra" and "gumbo" as synonymous. The little green pods have an ability to thicken whatever liquid they're cooked in, making gumbo a unique cross between a soup and a stew. Alternative ways to thicken gumbo include making a traditional roux out of white flour and butter or using a dash of filé powder. (Filé is the ground leaves of sassafras trees.) But the easiest option is to stir some chopped okra into your gumbo and let the pods do their magic.

Ghee for cooking
1 yellow onion, chopped
1 green or red bell pepper, stem and seeds removed, flesh chopped
4 ribs celery, trimmed and chopped
6 cups (48 ounces [1.4 L]) vegetable or seafood broth
15 ounces (411 g) diced canned tomatoes
2 bay leaves
2 teaspoons (2 g) thyme
2 teaspoons (1 g) basil
1 teaspoon sage
2 teaspoons (2 g) oregano
Dash Aleppo or cayenne pepper
½ cup (93 g) short-grain brown rice*
8 ounces (224 g) fresh or frozen okra, coarsely chopped (it's easiest to use already-chopped frozen okra)
2 cups (280 g) frozen corn
12 ounces (336 g) lump crab meat, drained
Pumpkin seed oil for garnishing

In a large soup pot, melt a generous knob of ghee over medium heat. Stir in the onion, bell pepper and celery. Sauté for 5 minutes or until the veggies are softened. Add the broth, tomatoes, herbs, Aleppo and rice.

Bring to a boil, and then reduce the heat to medium-low and simmer, covered, for 30 minutes. Uncover and increase the heat to medium. Stir in the okra, corn and crab. As soon as the gumbo comes to a boil, reduce the heat to medium-low and continue cooking uncovered for another 10 minutes or until the rice has reached the desired tenderness. If you'd like the crab to be chunky, wait until just before serving to stir in the crab meat.

When serving, drizzle each portion with a splash of pumpkin seed oil. Leftover gumbo can be refrigerated for 4 days.

*For a Paleo-friendly dish, substitute 1 small head of cauliflower (florets only; cut into bite-sized pieces) for the rice and use 4 cups (960 ml) of broth rather than 6 cups (1.4 L). The cauliflower only needs to simmer for 5 minutes, so add it with the okra, corn and crab, and don't add the final 2 cups (480 ml) of broth, and simmer the gumbo for 5 minutes or until the cauliflower has reached its desired tenderness.

Acknowledgments

If it takes a village to raise a child, it takes two villages to see a book to fruition. My heartfelt acknowledgments go to the people who helped make this book happen: Thanks to the Lisa Ekus Group team of Lisa, Sally, Jaimee and Samantha for being so endlessly enthusiastic and delightfully professional; to Will, Marissa and the entire creative team at Page Street for believing in the message and importance of this book; and to my parents for always expecting me to do my best, an attitude that has instilled me with a *carpe diem*! sort of spirit. Extra thanks to my mom for teaching me about the culinary world. As I like to put it, I attended the School of Mom.

And of course, a giant thanks also to the Fabulous Fifteen, a.k.a. my team of recipe testers. They include Michael and André, whose unwavering support for my "Go unrefined!" oil ideas is evinced by their own burgeoning collection of unprocessed oils; Lauryn, Karen M. and Jennifer, who join me every month in the kitchen to field-test my concoctions (*Bûche de Noël*, anyone?); Tanya, who, as one of my chief inspirations for exploring the gluten-free world, helped catapult me on my quality-first journey; Pauline and Deborah, culinary colleagues who selflessly share their ideas and motivations and help me feel like I'm part of something bigger; Debbie and Shawn, who—through a blend of gardening, hunting, cooking and just being darned fun people—are one of the most inspiring couples I know; Karen G., whose dining and dazzling company I've enjoyed for more than fifteen years (her kitchen feels like a second home!); Jill, who has lately begun to blaze her own culinary path after years of meat-and-potato-ing (I'm holding you to your "I will cook once a week" vow!); Jennie, who eagerly participated as a tester for both of my books despite the tester deadlines coinciding with things like getting married and attending law school; Dave, who undertakes cool culinary endeavors of his own, like making his own extracts and custom spirits; Adam, who is doubtless even more motivated in the kitchen now that he's a married man and can cook with his lovely (and culinarily talented) wife Priya; and of course, last but not least, my mom, who always has been and always will be my number-one cheerleader and inspiration. She also gives me tons of recipe ideas and proofreads every single blog post, magazine article and book manuscript I write, which makes her my unpaid-but-much-appreciated culinary and editorial staff. I couldn't do this without you, Mom!

About the Author

Culinary speaker, cooking instructor and recipe developer Lisa Howard is also the author of *Healthier Gluten-Free*. Through her recipes and classes, she loves to share the joy of food with others, and during her travels (she speaks German, Spanish and French) she explores new dishes and ingredients to share with audiences back home. She also helps her fellow eaters understand the connections between good food and good health.

Stop by her virtual kitchen at www.theculturedcook .com any time to check out more recipes and healthy tips. And if you happen to be in Metro Detroit, look for her wherever a Latin band is playing. When she's not in the kitchen, she's usually salsa dancing!

Index

Pan-Fried Rainbow Trout with Wilted
Spinach, Leeks and Hazelnut Oil,
162–63
heart attack risk, cholesterol and, 26
heat tolerance
choosing oils based on, 9, 34, 40, 42, 44
of specific oils, 24, 31, 34, 35, 36, 40, 43,
44, 46
hemp seed oil, 33, 39, 44, 190, 194
herbs. *See also specific herbs*
Herbed Brussels Sprouts Sautéed with
Chicken, Water Chestnuts and
Pomegranate Seeds, 164–65
Pecan-Crusted Salmon with Herb and Garlic
Rutabaga Oven Fries, 54–55
Pecan-Parmesan Crisps with Italian Herbs,
188
hydrogenated oils, 18

I
Ice Cream, Strawberry-Maple, with Toasted
Coconut and Walnut Oil, 196–97
inflammation, 20, 22, 23

J
Jambalaya, Shrimp and Bacon, with Cauliflower
Rice, 135
Jerk-Rubbed Chicken Rolled with Sun-Dried
Tomatoes, Ricotta and Spinach, 84–85

K
kabocha squash
Cardamom-Scented Lentils, Kabocha and
Lamb Sauté, 88–89
kabocha squash seed oil, 39, 44, 210
Kale, Beet and Cranberry Salad, Roasted Chicken
with, 186–87
Kelp Noodles, Szechuan Beef, Scallion and
Bamboo Stir-Fry with, 60–61
ketchup
Pork Burgers with Cilantro-Papaya Ketchup
with Mashed Yuca, 98–99
Keys, Ancel, 24–25
"knob" of ghee, meaning of, 46

L
label reading
for identifying trans fats, 18
for understanding oil descriptions, 27, 28,
29, 30, 31
lamb
Cardamom-Scented Lentils, Kabocha and
Lamb Sauté, 88–89

Coriander-Dusted Lamb Chops with
Sautéed Green Beans and Broccoli,
90–91
Gingered Sweet Potato Bisque with Lamb
and Spinach, 102–3
Lamb, Cashew and Sweet Potato Biryani
with Pistachio Oil, 176–77
Moroccan Harira with Lamb and Lentils,
120–21
Near East Jeweled Pilaf with Lamb, Carrots
and Sunchokes, 174–75
Roasted Peppers, Olives, Lamb and Mixed
Greens, 168–69
Rosemary, Lemon and Garlic Lamb with
Roasted Peas, Artichoke Hearts, Red
Onions and Carrots, 94–95
Slow-Cooked Lamb with Braised Fennel and
Smashed Rutabaga, 64–65
Sweet-and-Sour Lamb with Eggplant, Sweet
Potato and Cauliflower, 170–71
Thai Green Papaya Salad with Marinated
Lamb, 76–77
lard, 16, 36, 38
leeks
Pan-Fried Rainbow Trout with Wilted
Spinach, Leeks and Hazelnut Oil,
162–63
lemons
Baked Whitefish with Pineapple and Lemon
Salsa and Crispy Quinoa, 68–69
Citrusy Shrimp and Basil Spaghetti with
Macadamia Oil, 182–83
Rosemary, Lemon and Garlic Lamb with
Roasted Peas, Artichoke Hearts, Red
Onions and Carrots, 94–95
lentils
Cardamom-Scented Lentils, Kabocha and
Lamb Sauté, 88–89
Moroccan Harira with Lamb and Lentils,
120–21
Mushroom, Chorizo and Lentil Stir-Fry,
142–43
Za'atar-Spiced Green Wraps with Chicken,
Onions and Figs and Lentil-Yogurt
Dip, 178–79
Lettuce Tacos, Beef and Quinoa, with Fried
Avocado, 104–5
light and light-tasting oils, 31
limes
Chili-Lime Garlic Shrimp with Homemade
Guacamole, 152
Slow-Cooked Shredded Pork with Pineapple,
Lime and Macadamia Salsa and
Sweet Potato Crisps, 184–85
Lotus Chips, Deep-Fried, 156–57
low-fat diets, 14, 24–25

M
macadamia nut oil, 38, 44
Citrusy Shrimp and Basil Spaghetti with
Macadamia Oil, 182–83
Salmon, Sesame and Avocado Sushi Bowls
with Macadamia Nut Oil and
Shredded Daikon, 180–81
Slow-Cooked Shredded Pork with Pineapple,
Lime and Macadamia Salsa and
Sweet Potato Crisps, 184–85
macronutrients. *See* carbohydrates; fats; protein
Mahi-Mahi, Island Alfredo, with Amp-It-Up
Mango and Black-Eyed Pea Salad, 62–63
mangoes
Island Alfredo Mahi-Mahi with Amp-It-Up
Mango and Black-Eyed Pea Salad,
62–63
White Tuna Sautéed with Mango,
Mushrooms and Bok Choy, 204–5
maple syrup
Strawberry-Maple Ice Cream with Toasted
Coconut and Walnut Oil, 196–97
marinades, monounsaturated oils for, 170
meats. *See also* beef; bison; ham; lamb; pork;
prosciutto; salami
grass-fed vs. conventional, 10, 11, 23, 24
as protein source, 13
mesquite flour
Hazelnut Mesquite Brownies, 166–67
millet
Coffee, Coconut and Cocoa Granola, 153
monounsaturated fats, 16, 36. *See also* almond oil;
bacon drippings; hazelnut oil; macadamia
nut oil; olive oil; peanut oil; pecan oil;
pistachio oil; schmaltz
characteristics of, 38, 134
storing, 32, 33, 154
structure of, 17
swaps for, 44, 134
uses for, 134, 170
Muffaletta Scramble, New Orleans, 56–57
muffins
Butternut-Cashew Spiced Muffins, 51
Walnut-Raspberry Muffins, 146–47
mushrooms, 133
Hungarian-Inspired Mushroom, Beef and
Tomato Soup, 132–33
Mushroom, Chorizo and Lentil Stir-Fry,
142–43
White Tuna Sautéed with Mango,
Mushrooms and Bok Choy, 204–5